Work Matters

Work Matters

Lessons from Scripture

R. Paul Stevens

William B. Eerdmans Publishing Company
Grand Rapids, Michigan / Cambridge, U.K.

Published 2012 by
Wm. B. Eerdmans Publishing Co.
2140 Oak Industrial Drive N.E., Grand Rapids, Michigan 49505 /
P.O. Box 163, Cambridge CB3 9PU U.K.
www.eerdmans.com

Printed in the United States of America

18 17 16 15 14 13 12   7 6 5 4 3 2 1

Library of Congress Cataloging-in-Publication Data

Stevens, R. Paul, 1937-
Work matters: lessons from Scripture / R. Paul Stevens.
p.   cm.
Includes bibliographical references (p.   ).
ISBN 978-0-8028-6696-7 (pbk.: alk. paper)
1. Work — Biblical teaching.   2. Work — Religious aspects — Christianity.
3. Bible — Criticism, interpretation, etc.   4. Bible stories.   I. Title.

BS680.W75S74   2012
248.8′8 — dc23

2012003540

Contents

Foreword

The Christian faith, which arose as an extraordinary experience of the in-breaking of God's reign in history through Jesus Christ, was meant to be lived out in the midst of the world. Yet through the merging of many different intellectual and cultural currents, the call to bring God's life and justice to this world became relegated to the religious sphere of life and the rituals of the church. The extraordinary dualism between the spiritual and the secular that has so divided the Christian life for many people has had a devastating impact on those who try to live "in Christ" in every dimension of life.

The way out of this quagmire begins with reengaging the Bible from a different perspective; that is, by observing how God encounters his people and how they respond to him in the supposedly ordinary aspects of life. Little by little we begin to see what it means to live faithfully for him in every dimension of life, in every season of life. This will certainly involve the spiritual triad of "exercising faith," "extending love," and "bringing hope," but these spiritual practices are never isolated from the real stuff of everyday life.

In this extraordinary book, Paul Stevens captures this lived theology in the narratives of many of the best-known characters of the Bible. Each story builds upon itself as we move through the history of God's work in this world until we reach our final destiny in the new City of God. Woven throughout the book is a biblical theology of God's character and work demonstrated in creation, fall, redemption, and its final consummation. In short, this is both a systematic theology of vocation and a spiritual theology of personal transformation. Along the way we are provided with many insights regarding the importance and means of cultural engagement.

These insights into the biblical stories reflect a lifetime of engaging the text and seeking to apply it to the lives of people who work in the ordinary places of the world. Paul's reflections are consistently thoughtful, never trivial, often challenging, and always inspiring. That is to say, this is a book that engages both head and heart. I found it natural after each story to stop and ask: How does this change how I think about God, how he relates to his people and his world? And what does that mean for me today as I seek to live faithfully for him in the particularities of my life? Often I found the answers both provocative and enriching.

Don Flow
Chairman and CEO
Flow Automotive Companies
Chairman
Winston-Salem Business Inc.

Introduction

Before there was a theologian there was a storyteller. But, as it happens, the first storytellers in the Bible were also theologians. They explained the meaning of things in the light of God and his purposes for the world and humankind. The Bible is a collection of stories telling us of God's loving determination to renew everything, including people. As such it is rich in accounts of the lives and work of individuals whom God intended to be working models of the kingdom of God. All the way through the Bible we see workers and workplaces, some good and some bad, but all of them described in story form.

These stories, by and large, are not told with an explicit moralistic conclusion such as, "You must not do what so and so did" but are simply told in such a way that, when we see the consequences of how people acted and worked, we can know what bad work is like, and, by contrast, what good work is like. Sometimes, however, the story is accompanied by an inspired reflection on its implications.

Over the years my own work has included making steel rivets by hand, preaching, filing, attending committees, listening, building houses, teaching, writing, grading papers, and doing domestic work. Is some of this holy work, which will last into eternity, and is other work just fluff? What is good work? What is the point of this work? Who benefits? Does work have both intrinsic and extrinsic value? What does work mean? Whose work matters to God? These are some of the questions that must be answered by a theology of work. I am defining work as any purposeful expenditure of energy — whether manual, mental, or both, whether paid or not. Work is counterbalanced with leisure, rest, and Sabbath, though the line between them cannot always be drawn exactly. This is especially true for children, for whom work is play and play is work.

Toward a Theology of Work

The concept of a theology of work is a fairly recent development, entering Western thought after the Second World War, largely as a result of the work of Roman Catholic theologians.[1] Darrell Cosden describes this new discipline as "a theological exploration of work itself by exploring work with reference to a number of doctrines within a systematic theology."[2] Most attempts at elaborating a theology of work concentrate on *one* of those doctrines. Here is a partial list of those doctrines, with representative authors listed in the notes:

> *Trinitarian Theologies:* Work for human, God-imaging creatures is determined by the work of the Triune God.[3]
> *Creation Theologies:* Work was given in God's original design at the creation so that human beings could function as coworkers and co-creators with God.[4]

1. Darrell Cosden, *A Theology of Work: Work and the New Creation* (Carlisle, U.K.: Paternoster Press, 2004), pp. 4-5.
2. Cosden, *A Theology of Work,* p. 5.
3. Christian Schumacher, *God at Work: Discovering the Divine Pattern for Work in the New Millennium* (Oxford: Lion Publishing, 1998); Robert Banks, *God the Worker: Journeys into the Mind, Heart, and Imagination of God* (Valley Forge, Pa.: Judson Press, 1994); Gordon Preece, "The Three-Fold Call: The Trinitarian Character of Our Everyday Vocations," in Robert J. Banks, ed., *Faith Goes to Work: Reflections from the Marketplace* (Washington, D.C.: Alban Institute, 1993), pp. 160-71; David H. Jensen, *Responsive Labor: A Theology of Work* (Louisville: Westminster John Knox Press, 2006), pp. 43-66.
4. John C. Haughey, *Converting Nine to Five: A Spirituality of Daily Work* (New York: Crossroad, 1989); Doug Sherman and William Hendricks, *Your Work*

Image of God Theologies: God-imaging creatures are given power to make decisions and to make a difference.[5]

Curse Theologies: Work comes after the fall of human beings into sin and therefore is a negative thing and cursed.[6]

New Creation Theologies: Work is an expression of life under the New Covenant and therefore is both substantially redeemed and redeeming. We are coworkers with God in the new creation, collaborating with God in the creation of the world and embellishment of creation and human life. Some authors claim that toil and suffering in the context of our work actually contributes to our sanctification.[7]

Vocation Theologies: Work in our present situation is a calling of God.[8]

Matters to God (Colorado Springs: Navpress, 1987); Leland Ryken, *Work and Leisure in Christian Perspective* (Eugene, Ore.: Wipf and Stock Publishers, 1987); Joe Holland, *Creative Communion: Toward a Spirituality of Work* (New York: Paulist Press, 1989); John Paul II, *On Human Work (Laborem Exercens)* (Boston: Pauline Books & Media, n.d.); Paul Marshall, "Calling, Work, and Rest," in J. I. Packer, ed., *The Best in Theology* (Carol Stream, Ill.: Christianity Today, 1989), pp. 193-211; Gilbert C. Meilaender, ed., *Working: Its Meaning and Its Limits* (Notre Dame, Ind.: University of Notre Dame Press, 2000), pp. 25-48.

5. Dennis Bakke, *Joy at Work: A Revolutionary Approach to Fun on the Job* (Seattle: PVG, 2005); Raymond Bakke et al., *Joy at Work Bible Study Companion* (Seattle: PVG, 2005); Armand Larive, *After Sunday: A Theology of Work* (New York: Continuum, 2004).

6. Studs Terkel, *Working* (New York: Ballantine Books, 1974). Terkel's gift in coaxing narratives out of people shows that some of those interviewed who found deep meaning in their work are a counterpoise for his statement that "Jobs are not big enough for people." Jensen, *Responsive Labor;* Reg Theriault, *How to Tell When You're Tired: A Brief Examination of Work* (New York: W. W. Norton & Co., 1995); Jeremy Rifkin, *The End of Work: The Decline of the Global Work-Force and the Dawn of the Post-Market Era* (London: Penguin Books, 2000).

7. Stefan Cardinal Wyszynski, *All You Who Labor: Work and the Sanctification of Daily Life* (Manchester, N.H.: Sophia Institute Press, 1995); see also R. Bakke et al., *Joy at Work Bible Study Companion.*

8. Douglas J. Schuurman, *Vocation: Discerning Our Callings in Life* (Grand Rapids: Eerdmans, 2004); John Ting, *Living Biblically at Work* (Singapore: Landmark Books, 1995); Lee Hardy, *The Fabric of This World: Inquiries into Calling, Ca-*

Spirit Theologies: Work is an expression of the Spirit's work and giftedness, not only in church ministry but also in the world.[9]

Kingdom Theologies: Work is part of expressing God's life-giving and shalom-bringing rule over all of life, not only in the life to come but also in the present world.[10]

Heaven and End Times Theologies: The meaning of work is determined by the end. Some of our work in this life will last beyond the grave. The ultimate experience of work will be in the new heaven and new earth.[11]

This book is an approach to a comprehensive biblical theology of work. It constitutes a *theology* of work because it explains what work *means.* It is *biblical* because it draws on the entire Scripture, from Genesis to Revelation, by telling the stories of people — people like Adam and Eve, Ruth, David, Jesus, Paul, and John. In the process we see work illustrated in a variety of contexts within biblical history. At the same time we uphold the fundamental unity of Scripture.[12]

In this volume each major section of the Hebrew Bible — the Pentateuch, the historical books, the wisdom books, the prophets — and of the Christian Scriptures — the Gospels, the letters, and

---

reer Choice, and the Design of Human Work (Grand Rapids: Eerdmans, 1990); Paul S. Minear, "Work and Vocation in Scripture," in J. O. Nelson, ed., *Work and Vocation* (New York: Harper, 1954), pp. 32-115; Gordon Preece, *Changing Work Values: A Christian Response* (Melbourne: Acorn Press, 1995); Marshall, "Calling, Work, and Rest," in Packer, ed., *The Best in Theology,* pp. 193-211; Meilaender, ed., *Working,* pp. 104-25.

9. Miroslav Volf, *Work in the Spirit: Toward a Theology of Work* (New York: Oxford University Press, 1991); Rich Marshall, *God @ Work: Discovering the Anointing for Business* (Shippensburg, Pa.: Destiny Image Publishers, 2000).

10. Ben Witherington III, *Work: A Kingdom Perspective on Labor* (Grand Rapids: Eerdmans, 2011).

11. Cosden, *A Theology of Work;* Darrell Cosden, *The Heavenly Good of Earthly Work* (Peabody, Mass.: Henrickson, 2006); Paul Marshall, *Heaven Is Not My Home: Learning to Live in God's Creation* (Nashville: Word, 1998).

12. Glen Smith, "Theology at Work in Francophone Urban Contexts" (unpublished report for Bakke Graduate University, 2009), p. 1.

the Revelation — is briefly introduced and then followed by stories of people in the Bible who are workers. Discussion and reflection questions at the end of each chapter can be used in study and discussion groups. Summaries of each major portion of Scripture can be found at the end of each part. The epilogue reflects on how we should work in light of the preceding discussion.

A Kingdom Perspective on Work

Some have argued that we read the Bible the wrong way — from Genesis to Revelation rather than the other way around.[13] But we must remember that the whole revelation of Scripture points to the full coming of the kingdom of God, God's gracious and life-giving dynamic rule in people and in all things. So, instead of always looking back to the utopian sanctuary of the garden in Genesis as our ultimate destination, the Bible points to the final vision of the Garden-City in the new heaven and new earth in a totally transformed creation. We move forward in biblical revelation, not backward.

A simple analogy may help. When my wife thinks about an imminent birthday party for one of our eight grandchildren, her first thought is about the celebration event. Then she goes to the store and buys the elements for making a birthday cake, whips them up in the kitchen, cooks the cake in the oven, ices it, and then, with candles and songs, presents it to the birthday child. But the first thought was the party. And it seems that the whole biblical revelation points to this: God's first thought was the marriage supper of the Lamb, the final rendezvous of God, creation, and humankind. And to get there he made a world, made God-imaging creatures, and even sent his Son to redeem everything.

13. Criticism is sometimes made of Alan Richardson, *The Biblical Doctrine of Work* (London: SCM Press, 1954), which takes this approach. This work has never been updated. While contemporary authors on the theology of work draw on the biblical record, none since Richardson has attempted a comprehensive biblical overview.

But the end of it all — and what a glorious metaphor this is for the kingdom of God — is a party. While following the order of the books of the Bible in our study, we must bear in mind that the ultimate goal makes everything different, including our everyday work. Some have called this a kingdom perspective on work.[14]

The kingdom is essentially the spread of the goodness and shalom of God in the world and in human life. Drawing on the teachings of Vatican II, Russ Barta, founding president of the National Center for the Laity, says, "Our earthly task is to marry and beget, to establish civilizations and cultures, to create cities and industries, to search relentlessly for justice in institutions, to pursue the mysteries of life scientifically and philosophically, to fashion the best in the arts, to mediate harmony among people."[15] That is kingdom work.

What will be obvious as you read this book is that I have not covered everything in the Bible. Several volumes would be needed for this. The selection I have made is based on my reading of the Bible and brooding on what this means to everyday life. I have also had the privilege of teaching a theology of work at Regent College, Vancouver; at the Bakke Graduate University, Seattle; and in various settings in Asia, Africa, Central Europe, and South America. I acknowledge my indebtedness to others who have taught me and to those who have read this manuscript and made helpful comments, especially my colleague Sven Soderlund, who has patiently and carefully edited the manuscript. I have left some quotations as they stand where "man" or "men" is used even though human beings male and female is implied and intended. Elsewhere I have tried to make this document as inclusive as possible including the use of an inclusive Bible translation.

Enjoy, but more than that. Discover a new work-view that can revolutionize not only our own work life but the mission of the people of God in the world. In an early English-language survey of the biblical teaching on work, Paul S. Minear points to the

14. See Witherington, *Work*.

15. Bill Droel, *Initiatives: In Support of Christians in the World* (Chicago: National Center for the Laity, September 2007), p. 4.

transformative implications of a biblical theology of work. "It is this revolution which the Reformation partially re-enacted, and which may yet again in our own day break out with its pristine power."[16]

16. Minear, "Work and Vocation in Scripture," in Nelson, ed., *Work and Vocation,* pp. 67-68.

PART ONE

God-Given Work

An Introduction to the First Five Books

The Bible is "an album of casual photographs of labor-
ers. . . . A book by workers, about workers, for workers —
that is the Bible."

Paul Minear, "Work and Vocation in Scripture"

Genesis opens with God at work, the first and finest worker in the universe. Theologian David Jensen notes how radical this is:

God does not sit enthroned in heaven removed from work, willing things into existence by divine fiat. Unlike the gods of the Greco-Roman mythologies, who absolve themselves of work — dining on nectar and ambrosia in heavenly rest and contemplation — the biblical God works. This God molds humans in God's image, establishes covenant with a displaced people, laments when the covenant is broken, strives to re-establish covenant with that people, and becomes incarnate to labor, suffer, die, and be raised for the whole world.[1]

1. David H. Jensen, *Responsive Labor: A Theology of Work* (Louisville: Westminster John Knox Press, 2006), p. 22.

God the Worker

The Bible shows that God is still working (John 5:17) in contrast to one popular perception that now that God has gotten everything running he is resting eternally. Throughout the Bible we see different images of God as a worker, such as gardener (Gen. 2:8), shepherd (Ps. 23), potter (Jer. 18:6), physician (Matt. 8:16), teacher (Ps. 143:10), vineyard-dresser (Isa. 5:1-7), and metalworker and refiner (Mal. 3:2-3; Ezek. 22:20), to name only a few. These are all rich metaphors drawn from almost every trade, craft, and role in human experience. God is as active and creative today — creating, sustaining, redeeming, and consummating — as he was when he began to make this vast universe. But there is more.

Later in the Bible we discover that God is a being in communion. Unpacking this biblical truth is life-giving and also work-informing. Long ago St. Augustine said that God is lover, beloved, and love itself. To say that "God is love" (1 John 4:16) is not merely to give an important attribute to God, but rather to say that God is God in loving, in constant self-giving, and in receiving. God is also sender, sent, and sending, constantly going outside of himself in creating, working, and transforming.[2] The Father exists and works in relation to the Son and the Spirit, each revealing the other, each bringing a distinctive emphasis to the work of God.[3] God is three persons in a social unity, each for the other and all for the One, so deeply united that God is truly "one" God. At the core of reality is personhood. God is the most personal being in the universe. Human beings are "like" God in being relational ("in the image of God he created them; male and female he created them," Gen. 1:27). So our fundamental human vocation is to be people-prizing and people-keeping. But there is another way in which we are like God.

---

2. See John 4:34; 5:24; 14:26; 15:26; 17:18; 20:21. There are references to sending within God and by God thirty-one times in the Gospel of John.

3. Matt. 11:27; John 10:30; 14:9-10, 16-17, 23; 2 Thess. 2:13-17; Eph. 2:19-22.

Human Beings as Coworkers with God

We are also made in the image of God as workers. We are called to work as God does (Gen. 1:28), and that calling does not stop at sixty-five or some arbitrary retirement age. Our work involves being vice-regents over creation. We are commanded to act as stewards of God's created world. In some religions where matter is deified, humans do not enjoy the same dignity and cannot exercise the same responsibility because the material world itself is meant to be worshiped. But creation is neither a curse nor an idol. It is a wonderful reality with the signature of God on it, and a reality on which humankind is also to write its signature through being world-makers, culture-makers, tool-makers, community-makers, and beauty-makers.

As we will see, work is good. It is intrinsically good, which means that work is good in itself. It is also extrinsically good — good for what it produces and what it leads to. In the first few chapters of Genesis, Adam and Eve were placed in a sanctuary garden, an environment of beauty, prosperity, and safety. But these first human beings were commissioned to fill the whole earth. The Genesis account suggests concentric circles of reality. First there is the garden, a sanctuary of beauty, pleasure, and prosperity, where Adam and Eve were placed. But the next circle is Eden. The garden is "in Eden" (Gen. 2:8), Adam and Eve's home. But beyond Eden are the other lands like Havilah (Gen. 2:11-12), suggestive of the larger world. Adam and Eve were prototype human beings called to extend the sanctuary (the garden) into the world. They were to "fill" it not only by populating the earth, but by filling it in such a way as to humanize the earth and develop it in a way that brought glory to God through procreativity and co-creativity. As God delighted in his creation (Gen. 1:31), humans too find fulfillment when they do good work.

The two words used by God in his command (Gen. 2:15) for Adam to work are *abad* (work) and *shamar* (take care). Interestingly, these words are also used to mean "service to God" and "keeping of his commandments," respectively. This implies that we should make no distinction between sacred and secular work.

In God's design there is no dualism — sacred and secular. At least that is true of good work. But there is also bad work. Trouble came.

The Growth Test

No one grows without testing. Adam and Eve were challenged to choose whether they would live in dependence on God or in autonomy (Gen. 3). Their eating from the autonomy tree — the tree of the knowledge of good and evil — led not only to shame, separation from God, and alienation between the man and woman, but to the degradation of work, the worker, and the workplace. The woman experiences the curse primarily in terms of relationships, especially with her husband, while the man experiences the curse primarily in terms of his work. This raises a fascinating question of whether men and women experience work differently, and whether they bring to work different gifts, something we will explore later.

Note that the command to work was given *before* the fall and hence work is meant to be a blessing, not a curse. Toil, bad work, and the idolatry of work are the *results* of the fall. The suspicion with which many people regard vocations in the marketplace undoubtedly comes from the fact that some work is driven by selfish ambition for wealth, power, or money, as was the case with the Tower of Babel (Gen. 11). But work is not essentially sinful. In fact, the determination of God to redeem work and workers starts in the garden in Eden and continues through the whole biblical story, especially as the Trinitarian character of God is revealed.

The Trinity and Human Work

The relational character of God has implications for work. First, human work, shaped by the Triune God, is essentially personal. Just as each person of the Trinity brings otherness and difference — origin, implementation, and empowerment — to the unity of

God, so each human being has a distinctive work to bring to the world.[4] Workers are not interchangeable cogs in a vast cosmic machine or even in human corporations. Second, human work is God-like when it is relational. This means that we are designed to work together; each person's work is to be enriched by and intended to enrich his or her neighbor. For some of the earliest formulators of the doctrine of the Trinity, the Cappadocian Fathers of the Eastern church, relationship is the chief marker of personhood. Each person is an inseparable part of the others.[5] David Jensen describes this beautifully: "The work of creating, redeeming, and transforming the world is not a one-time fiat of a divine monarch or the result of three separate decrees, but a movement of distinctive personal work sustained by a community of love."[6] Gone, or rather, never to have been invented in the first place, is a hierarchy of occupations with the pastor and people-helping professionals at the top and the ditch digger and stock broker at the bottom. Each person has something to give and each person needs others to complete his or her own work. This is something revealed throughout the Bible's first five books and the stories of workers contained in these accounts.

Other Workers Good and Bad

Genesis continues to tell us about other workers: Cain; the people who made the Tower of Babel; Abraham and Sarah, who were the first missionary workers; Jacob, the herdsman in the far country; Joseph, who as a believer in the one God ended up running all of Egypt as second-in-command to Pharaoh. Then, in Exodus, the second of the "five books," Moses led the Hebrew people out of an alienating and violent work situation in Egypt and received God's

4. See Christian Schumacher, *God in Work* (Oxford: Lion Publishing House, 1998), and Jensen, *Responsive Labor,* pp. 43-66.

5. The Greek word that is used to describe this is *perichoresis,* a relatedness that involves reciprocity but not monarchy.

6. Jensen, *Responsive Labor,* p. 52.

Ten Commandments, which include a commandment directly about work, namely that it is limited by Sabbath, and another about the spirituality of work — that is, the command not to covet what your neighbor has or does. The Ten Commandments also contain a number of injunctions that bear on work, such as the commands to be truthful and not harm one's neighbor. Exodus describes people working in the wilderness, including one character, Bezalel, who is the only person in the Old Testament of whom it is said that he was "filled . . . with the Spirit of God" (Exod. 31:3). Already we can see that the redemption of work does not begin with the coming of Jesus but is found as far back as the garden in Eden and progresses continuously through the story.

Leviticus, the third of the five books, describes many aspects of the lifestyle of God's chosen people, including how to provide work for the poor (Lev. 19:9-10). Leviticus also describes the fifty year celebration — the Jubilee — through which the fruits of work gained at the expense of others are to be returned to the original workers by restoring family land (25:8-17). Numbers, the fourth book, besides naming and numbering the people of God and documenting their journey in the wilderness in those early days, contains many stories of people living and working righteously and also, sadly, in unrighteous ways. The fifth book, Deuteronomy, is essentially a renewal of the covenant, the binding agreement between God and the people to belong to each other. Deuteronomy contains many expressions of a redemptive approach to work: provision for cancelling the debts of people hopelessly in economic bondage, prohibition against charging interest to one's own people, the first building code requiring a railing around a balcony, care of slaves, honest weights and measures, and provision for the poor by leaving the edges of the field for gleaning (Deut. 15–25). Included in the legislation and the several work stories is the description of the ideal king who, unlike so many CEOs today, does not enrich himself through his position, is sexually and financially faithful, and does not think of himself as better than others (17:14-20).

In the following five chapters we will look in more detail at some of the topics surveyed in this introduction to the first five books. As we will see, the first five books are crucial for gaining a biblical perspective on work, especially as we now turn to the story of the creation of the man and woman made in the image of God.

1

Good Work — Adam and Eve

When does a job feel meaningful? Whenever it allows us to generate delight or reduce suffering in others. Though we are often taught to think of ourselves as inherently selfish, the longing to act meaningfully in our work seems just as stubborn a part of our make-up as our appetite for status or money.

Alain de Bottom, *The Pleasures and Sorrows of Work*

As we have seen, the Bible opens with God at work making things — both separating and filling. For instance, God separated light and darkness and then filled them with meaning, calling them night and day. This is a story about something that really happened. It is not myth or parable, but it is written in such a way that the simplest Bedouin nomad and today's most sophisticated nuclear physicist could grasp the point that God is the Creator, that God makes everything beautiful (the meaning of "it is good") and that he himself is the author of work.

Work as an Expression of Covenant

The first chapter of Genesis, however, is placed within the larger story of God's covenant relationship with creation, with people in general, and with God's promised people in particular.[1] Covenant is a relationship of belonging, expressed in the covenant formula, "You will be my people, and I will be your God" (Jer. 30:22).[2] It is like the promises made in the marriage ceremony: "You are mine. I am yours." *Covenant* contrasts with *contract*. A contract is an agreement to exchange goods and services upon some predetermined terms. A covenant is essentially relational. So the meaning of God's superlative creativity is that God *belongs* to what he has made and what he has made belongs to God. The whole of the created order, and of humankind in particular, is an expression of the imagination of God.[3] This is especially true of the climax of God's creativity — a creature that resembles himself (Gen. 1:26) — with the result that humans are an external expression of an internal image. Paraphrasing a statement by the theologian Karl Barth, covenant fidelity is "the inner meaning and purpose of our creation as human beings in the divine image." Instead of work being, as is so often said, part of the "creation mandate" to take care of the earth, work is part of the *covenant mandate*. It is part of what it means to belong to God, to honor God, and to invest in God's purposes. Work is not a human invention. It is a divine calling and a way of imitating and resembling our Creator. To be made in the image of God means that we are created like God as relational beings and that we are made like God in that we work.

Work is not easily defined. Some have defined it as energy expended purposively, whether manual, mental, or both, but nonetheless it is purposeful energy that brings glory to God and serves our neighbor. This is not a bad definition of "good" work. But unfortunately a lot of bad work in the world deconstructs creation, abuses our neighbor, and does not bring glory to God. But what God had in mind when he called and commissioned his creatures, both Adam and Eve, was certainly for them to engage

---

1. William Dumbrell, "Creation, Covenant and Work," *Crux* 24, no. 3 (September 1988): 14-24.

2. See also Exod. 19:8; Deut. 10:12-22.

3. See Robert Banks, *God the Worker: Journeys into the Mind, Heart and Imagination of God* (Valley Forge, Pa.: Judson Press, 1994).

in good work: "Be fruitful and increase in number; fill the earth and subdue it. Rule over the fish in the sea and the birds in the sky and over every living creature that moves on the ground" (Gen. 1:28). God said this to human beings in the context of blessing: "God blessed them and said. . . ." And afterwards his first offer of something good to the mandated human beings was the gift of food. God saw everything that he had made and said, "Beautiful."

Filling the Earth and World-Making

The human calling in Genesis is not merely to work but that calling has three dimensions: to commune with God — the sanctuary garden; to build community — "male and female he made them"; and to co-create with God. This is the covenant mandate. Adam and Eve soon messed this up but not irrevocably, as we shall see. Even though human beings have fallen, even though the "image" has been distorted, and even though, from the perspective of the New Testament, substantial redemption has come in Christ — though it will not completely come until the new heaven and new earth — nonetheless, work can be good. So what does all this mean for our understanding and practice of good work?

First, good work is a means of spiritual growth. People often think that work is a hindrance to spiritual growth. But work is it-self a spiritual discipline. The first challenge to Adam and Eve's spiritual growth, in this case the test to see whether they would eat from the tree of autonomy (called "the tree of the knowledge of good and evil" in the Bible), took place in the context of work — harvesting fruit. In a rare volume on the biblical doctrine of work, Alan Richardson reinforces this point. The human being "is so made that not only can he not satisfy his material needs without working but also he cannot satisfy his spiritual needs, or fulfill his function as a human being."[4] As a calling from God rather than a

---

4. Alan Richardson, *The Biblical Doctrine of Work* (London: SCM Press, 1954), p. 22.

human invention, good work is inspired by the goodness of God and directed to the pleasure of God.

Second, good work is communal. It is a means of building community and serving our neighbors. We are called to work *together,* in partnership. Work and its organizations impact social structures and the social order. We become who we are in relationship. We are full-time husbands and wives, full-time daughters and sons, full-time neighbors and full-time siblings. Human relationships and society become more fully realized through work. A "company" is literally a way of sharing bread — *cum pane,* that is, "with bread." This is true whether we are involved in making a meal, or making a deal; whether we are breaking ground for farming or inventing a new tool; whether we are teaching children or inspecting the town's water supply; whether we are building an office culture or creating a family. Good work is for the commonwealth, in the sense of the old English word that means for the "common good." Kenneth Kantzer notes how business is implicit in the creation of humankind as male and female: "By creation, human beings are social beings, never intended to live alone. Because of our social nature, we are specialized (each person is in one sense unique), interdependent and, therefore, necessarily dependent on exchange. Exchange is built into our very nature. And this *is* business."[5]

Third, good work unfolds the potential of creation. The best word to describe this is stewardship — that rich idea that we do not own anything but have been trusted with its care and development. I stress "development" because God never intended the entire globe to be kept as pure wilderness everywhere, as much as I love to canoe in the Canadian wilderness. The appointment of humans to "rule" (Gen. 1:26), given in the covenant, does not mean we can rapaciously exploit creation but it does mean that we have a limited sovereignty accountable to our Creator for our "care" of creation (2:15). We do this by making "worlds" — tools, culture, communities, beauty, homes, comfort, music, meaning,

---

5. Kenneth Kantzer, in Richard C. Chewning, ed., *Biblical Principles & Economics: The Foundations,* vol. 1 (Colorado Springs: Navpress, 1989), p. 24.

transportation, toys, accounts, communication, images, machines, health, gardens, research, and meaning. This is joint work with God — entering into God's ongoing work of creating, sustaining, transforming, and consummating, aptly expressed by Eve when she said, "With the help of the LORD I have brought forth a man" (Gen. 4:1). We are truly "conservatives." That word, which means to "serve jointly," suggests that the earth and living things serve us and we serve the earth and living things.

So listen to the story of Adam and find your story making sense within the grand story of God's creative purpose. Good work is energy expended purposively, to be distinguished from play, leisure, and Sabbath, whether that energy is manual, mental, or both, that brings glory to God, is a means of spiritual growth, builds community by serving our neighbor, and unfolds the potential of creation. In due course we will explore other stories in the Bible that elaborate what this work means and how we can undertake it.

For Discussion and Reflection

Review in detail the work you most commonly undertake, whether or not that work is paid. How do you go about it? With what materials do you work? How is this work a service to others, whether your neighbor is visible or not? In what ways do you see this work as entering into God's work?

2

Degraded Work — Cain

Work, for most of mankind, is something to avoid if possible. Not merely avoid but, if you are powerful enough or have money enough, arrange for someone else to do for you. Work always has to be done. Among those working people at the bottom of the labor heap, trapped in drudgery and perhaps powerless to escape, getting "promoted" to an easier job is never far from their minds.

Reg Theriault, *How to Tell When You're Tired:*
A Brief Examination of Work

Work is hard. Most of the time we do not find our work ecstatically joyful or our workplaces particularly enriching. We encounter not only difficult people and complex ethical problems but also invisible forces that attempt to control us negatively, the "principalities and powers" of mammon, greed, predatory competition, systemic unemployment, and the market. Even Scripture does not promise complete satisfaction until the *eschaton* when the realm of God fully comes. Why is this so? Something has happened — something that affects the worker, work, and the workplace. The story of Cain and his parents is critical to understanding this.

Adam and Eve, Cain's parents, were placed in a sanctuary garden and were given a choice. They could live autonomously, seeking work and the pleasures of the garden for their own sake and without any reference to God. Or they could live in loving obedience and communion with God in daily life. The tree of the knowledge of good and evil (see Gen. 2:17) represented the possibility of having provision ("good for food"), pleasure ("pleasing to the eye"), and power ("desirable for gaining wisdom") without God (Gen. 3:6). They chose "freedom" from God, only to discover bondage. And the results were extensive, both personally and relationally: loss of intimacy ("they realized they were naked" [3:7]), mutual blaming and shifting of responsibility ("the woman you put here with me, she . . ." [3:12]), and the politicization of relationships ("[your husband] will rule over you" [3:16]). But work was also affected. According to Genesis 3:16, work would now become sweaty and hard with the workplace infested with thorns and thistles, a poetic way of describing the troubles every worker in the world encounters. And with Cain, Adam and Eve's oldest son, the problem of the worker, work, and the workplace gets ratcheted up.

There Were a Man and Woman with Two Sons

In this descriptive account, the primal couple had two sons, Cain and Abel, each with a different skill. Already we are beginning to see the diversification of talent, gift, and calling, which tells us that all human life is based on relationship and exchange. Cain was a farmer and Abel was a herder. Still, they needed each other, just as punch press operators need grocers and university professors need auto technicians. In spite of their now dysfunctional family, the two offspring still wanted to combine work and worship — something anticipated in the Hebrew word for work, which also means worship. They offered the firstfruits of their work to God. There was nothing wrong with offering grain — Cain's offering — instead of meat — Abel's offering. But there was something wrong in Cain's heart. Scripture does not tell us what was wrong until we get to the New Testament, where the author of Hebrews 11:4 reveals that Abel brought his offering *with faith*, that is, as an expression of God-ward dependence and gratitude, all in the context of a relationship of loving awe that demonstrated his integration of work and spirituality. Cain, in contrast, did not make his offering "with faith."

God's approval of Abel and disapproval of Cain led to the pollution of Cain's work and the destruction of his relationship with his coworker, Abel. He was consumed by jealousy and anger. So he decided to eliminate the competition, just as Joseph's brothers were later to try to eliminate Jacob's favorite and privileged son Joseph. Competition in business and the workplace is not in itself evil or wrong. In fact, it can be a stimulus to creativity and initiative. But predatory competition is destructive because one's identity becomes wrapped up in eliminating the competitor. And that is precisely what Cain wanted to do.

Enter a gracious God. God pleaded with Cain that "sin is crouching at your door; it desires to have you, but you must master it" (Gen. 4:7). God offered Cain a way out, a way of acting righteously, a way of acceptance and approval. But Cain would not be persuaded — even by God. He refused to repent — even after he slaughtered his brother like one of Abel's cows; he would not be responsible — even after God graciously called to him, "Where is your brother?," reminiscent of God's call to Adam and Eve in Genesis 3:9. To God's question Cain replied, "Am I my brother's keeper?" (Gen. 4:9). As a result of his insolent reply, Cain was cursed. The ground would not yield its fruit; work would become frustrating. And Cain, the original *individual* who owed no responsibility or duty to anyone other than himself, became a wanderer on earth, the prototype of all homeless and lonely people.

But once again, God was gracious. God gave Cain a mark of protection so that anyone trying to kill him would suffer vengeance seven times over. Cain's descendant Lamech ups the ante and says that if Cain is avenged sevenfold, Lamech will be avenged seventy-seven times (Gen. 4:24). But from Cain's descendants also came civilization as we have come to know it: commerce — "those who live in tents and raise livestock"; culture — "all who play the harp and flute"; and crafts — "[those] who forged all kinds of tools out of bronze and iron" (Gen. 4:20-22).

All this good creativity and unfolding of creation's potential — something to which Adam and Eve had been summoned — is laced with frustration, predatory competition, soul-deadening sin, and people-destroying work environments. At the beginning of his well-known book on the nature of work in the American context, Studs Terkel said:

> This book, being about work, is, by its very nature, about violence — to the spirit as well as to the body. It is about ulcers as well as accidents . . . about nervous breakdowns as well as kicking the dog around. It is, above all (or beneath all), about daily humiliations. To survive the day is triumph enough for the walking wounded among the great many of us.[1]

The Globalization of Thorns and Thistles

The Industrial Revolution of the eighteenth and nineteenth centuries brought new "thorns and thistles." The unwelcome by-products of that "revolution" have included narrowness and monotony of tasks; the inability to see an overall purpose in one's isolated task; the denial of satisfaction that comes from the complexity in work; the depersonalized and anonymous nature of work; and the lack of a sense of participation and pride in one's work. All too familiar in the workplaces of the world are power struggles, exploitation, and injustice. The Information or so-called Creativity Society has brought its own challenges: information overload and rapidly escalating pressure to be continuously creative. But today, with the added dimension of globalization, the thorns and thistles have grown out of control. Or so it seems.

Globalization can be defined as the intensification of worldwide social relations, which links distant localities in such a way that local happenings are shaped by events occurring many miles

---

1. Studs Terkel, *Working: People Talk about What They Do All Day and How They Feel about What They Do* (New York: Ballantine Books, 1974), p. xiii.

away and vice versa. International development philosophies demonstrate this, and globalization is represented in the World Bank, the International Money Fund, and the transfer of weaponry and war technology. It is then disseminated by information technology through the Internet and the globalization of pop culture, all too often from the West. All of this is a mixed blessing. On the one hand, God intended the earth to be filled with a grand international and intercultural community of peoples. But instead of a rich unity *through diversity* a homogenization of culture and commerce has arisen, of which the Tower of Babel is the biblical symbol: all speaking the same language and making a name for themselves. So God's descent to the city to confuse the languages and scatter the people (Gen. 11:1-9) was both judgment and fulfillment: judgment for their arrogant and autonomous pride, and fulfillment in forcing them to "fill the earth."

So the global workplace has its own thorns and thistles. Currently we are experiencing unemployment in both highly industrialized and less industrialized countries, damage to the biosphere, loss of community, crisis of cultural identity, and labor concerns, especially in relation to the conditions and terms of work. In a huge Chinese factory that manufactures most of the world's computer parts, young men and women were hurling themselves to death because of the meaninglessness of their all-consuming work. The owner tried to solve the problem by stretching safety nets between the workers' high-rise dorms![2]

Three fundamental problems of global capitalism are the globalization of poverty, hyper-resource consumption, and economic alienation from transcendent norms. No longer restrained by the Protestant work ethic, global capitalism feeds on greed or fear, depending on the wind-shifts of the market. "Capitalism," says Os Guiness, "having defeated all challenges, such as socialism, now faces its greatest challenge — itself, because it devours the very virtues it needs to thrive."[3]

2. www.bbc.co.uk/news/10182824

3. Os Guiness, *The Call: Finding and Fulfilling the Central Purpose of Your Life* (Nashville: Word, 1998), p. 135.

Is God in globalization? Yes and no.[4] God is in the process providentially. The social-cultural forces most often identified with globalization developed in societies fundamentally stamped by Christian theological ethics. But globalization is not the realm of God. Nor will it bring in the realm. On the other hand, globalization can be an opportunity to work and serve towards the vision of the New Jerusalem.

Thorns and thistles will exist until Christ comes again and brings the whole human story to a wonderful fulfillment, but in the meantime we must not take our cues from the past in the fall or from a utopian garden before the fall, but we must be empowered by the future, the eternity that is infiltrating the thorns and thistles of this world now.

For Discussion and Reflection

What are the "thorns and thistles" in your daily work and in your work environment? The Canadian theologian Paul Marshall asserts that the scope of redemption in Christ is the same as the scope of creation. In what way could you begin to see the redemption of your work and workplace?

---

4. See Vinay Samuel, "Evangelical Response to Globalisation: An Asian Perspective," *Transformation* (January 1999), and Max L. Stackhouse and Peter Paris, eds., *God and Globalization: Religion and the Powers of the Common Life,* vol. 1 (Harrisburg, Pa.: Trinity Press International, 2000).

3

Virtuous Work — Jacob

O Lord our heavenly Father, by whose providence the duties
of men are variously ordered: grant to us all the spirit to la-
bor heartily to do our work in our several stations, in serv-
ing one Master and looking for one reward. Amen.

The Book of Common Prayer

Jacob is sometimes called the first worker in the Bible — the first
to have his work vividly described in its complexities and satisfactions (Gen. 29:14-20; 31:10-13). But more important, this story reveals God's interest in work. Jacob's work (and ours) is a way to
God; it is blessed by God and becomes a ministry to God and our
neighbor. This is all the more remarkable when one considers that
Jacob's work was slave work — which is exactly how many will describe their work today: routine, monotonous, never-ending, in-
adequately remunerated, exhausting, and just plain hard.[1]

Jacob arrives in Paddan Aram penniless, running from his
brother and searching for a wife from the extended family home.
But his father did not send him with the bride price. He has
nothing to give for Rachel, the gorgeous lady at the well, but his

---

1. Much of this chapter was originally published in R. Paul Stevens, *Down-
to-Earth Spirituality: Encountering God in the Ordinary, Boring Stuff of Life*
(Downers Grove, Ill.: InterVarsity Press, 2003), pp. 92-102. Permission granted.

sweat. So it appears he effectively indentured himself as a slave to Laban to get Rachel — working for seven years with no pay, no freedom, and no dignity. He looks after his future father-in-law's animals.

When Jacob describes his work, he uses the language of slaves. "Sleep fled from my eyes," he says (31:40). "The heat consumed me in the daytime and the cold at night" (31:40). Later he complains to Laban, "You changed my wages ten times" (31:41).[2] He describes his work as "my hardship and the toil of my hands" (31:42).

Love Work

The surprising reversal in the story is an eruption of hope and good news, a breaking in of a God-sized view of work. In Genesis 29:20 we have one of the purest statements of human love: "So Jacob served seven years to get Rachel, but they seemed like only a few days to him because of his love for her." Slave work can become love work. Love transforms all kinds of work into ministry.

Working for the love of a woman or a man, for one's parents or children, for one's neighbor, for love of the earth, for love of nation and love of God — any of this can transform work into a ministry. And in the last day Jesus will say, in effect, "You changed my diapers, you visited me in prison, you made my dinner, you hosted me at a business reception, you put clothes on my back." And then the parable concludes, "Whatever you did for one of the least of these brothers and sisters of mine, you did for me" (Matt. 25:40, TNIV). Jesus (yes, God) receives our work, and not just religious work such as preaching, pastoral care, church planting, and other types of formal ministry.

In 1 Thessalonians 1:3 Paul wrote to the Christians saying, "We continually remember before our God and Father your work produced by faith, your labor prompted by love, and your endur-

2. If Jacob got a lot of spotted animals for himself, Laban would say, "Let's make your wages the striped ones." But Jacob got striped ones in a big way. And on it went.

ance inspired by hope in our Lord Jesus Christ." Jacob worked for love, but did he work with faith?

Faith Work

After fourteen years Jacob wants to do something for his own family. He has paid off the bride price (actually for two wives!); now he wants to work for wages. So he negotiates with Laban for a few more years of work. Their conversation is a masterpiece of diplomacy. Laban asks, "What shall I give you?" (30:31) but really doesn't want to give him anything. Jacob knows a cheat when he sees one, so he says, "Don't give me anything." But Jacob shrewdly offers a plan that would enable Laban not to give him anything but that at the same time (though Jacob does not reveal this) would enable Jacob to get what he needs for his family.

What happens is brilliant — entrepreneurial but surprisingly inspired by faith. The results are not guaranteed, so Jacob must trust. But it is not a blind trust, a leap in the dark. God gives him an idea. Children of our creative God are inspired by the Holy Spirit. They should be the most creative people on earth — and not just in church work, but in world-making work.[3]

What happens next is shrewd, the kind of business deal that would make the toughest worldling admit that it ought to be commended (Luke 16:8). It is also mysterious, perhaps even magical. Jacob's work has been shepherding and he has noticed that the sheep are mostly all white and the goats are mostly all black. Multi-colored animals are rare. He makes an offer that Laban cannot refuse and he strategizes how to make it impossible for himself not to lose. Today we would call it win-win.

Jacob proposes that Laban will keep all the pure white sheep and pure black goats and also the presently living mixed-color animals. What Jacob will take for his own wages will be all *future*

---

3. For a theology and spirituality of entrepreneurship see Paul Stevens, "Spiritual and Religious Sources of Entrepreneurship: From Max Weber to the New Business Spirituality," *Crux* 36, no. 2 (June 2000): 22-33.

multi-colored lambs or kids.[4] For the present, Jacob will separate out all multi-colored ones for Laban to keep. Laban, like Jacob, knows a cheat when he sees one, so he does not trust Jacob with the separation of the flocks. So Laban separates out the multi-colored flocks, takes them three days' journey away, and puts them in the care of Laban's own sons (30:35-36). Effectively, Laban has everything. He has all the animals — the blacks, the whites, and the (present) multi-colored ones. He has Jacob to care for some of his flocks, and Jacob's chances of generating a nest egg for his family are a remote possibility, or so Laban thinks. Such a deal! "Don't give me anything" (v. 31), Jacob explains. But Jacob has a plan.

Jacob could not have understood the principles of genetics, namely that recessive genes may emerge through mating. But his observations as a shepherd led him to believe that he could breed strong, *multi-colored* animals in a big way through careful selective breeding. And he could do this with all-white and all-black animals (since Laban already had the first batch of multi-colored ones and Jacob was still taking care of Laban's monochrome animals). Some research indicates that the vigorous animals are hybrids "whose recessive coloring genes emerge when they are bred together" and that "Jacob can distinguish the strong animals with the recessive genes by their copulating earlier than the weaker ones without that gene."[5]

Here is where it gets mysterious as well as cunning. He does this by something that might be a primitive magic, by placing a multi-colored post in front of the animals while they are mating, on the assumption that what they see during intercourse determines their own color (30:37-40). The upshot is clear. Jacob succeeds in breeding multi-colored sheep and goats from monochrome stock and ensures that the strongest sheep and goats are the multi-colored

---

4. Wenham notes that Jacob's offer is certainly less than the typical twenty percent of newborn lambs or kids that ancient shepherds received for their wages. Gordon Wenham, *Genesis 16–50*, Word Biblical Commentary, vol. 2 (Dallas: Word, 1994), p. 256.

5. Bruce K. Waltke, *Genesis: A Commentary* (Grand Rapids: Zondervan, 2001), p. 420. Waltke bases his thoughts on N. Sarna's research in his commentary, *Genesis*, JPS Torah Commentary, 1989.

ones — in other words, his! The narrator concludes: "In this way the man grew exceedingly prosperous and came to own large flocks, and female and male servants, and camels and donkeys" (v. 43, TNIV). Not surprisingly, Laban the out-foxed fox changed his attitude to Jacob (31:1-2) and it was time for Jacob to leave. Jacob's plan is brilliantly entrepreneurial. But where is God in this? Is there merely unbridled selfish ambition, a work of the flesh (Gal. 5:20)?

Six years later Jacob recalls a dream he had received from God. As he sensitively and diplomatically draws his wives into the country to discuss in secret his desire to leave Haran and return to Canaan, he uses a multifaceted strategy. He notes that Laban's attitude has changed. He recalls how hard he has worked and how their father has cheated him. Then he appeals to divine providence: "God has taken away your father's livestock and has given them to me" (31:9). Finally he tells them what we have not known up to this point — that God gave him a dream that offered the secret of his success in animal husbandry. God showed him that the strong animals mating were striped, spotted, and speckled.

Jacob is working out of faith and holy ambition. He has been doing "the Lord's work" on his father-in-law's ranch. In the same way we work in faith when we honor the ideas that God gives us and work to please God. Jacob's approach to work is an Old Testament hint of Paul's advice: "Whatever you do, work at it with all your heart, as working for the Lord, not for human masters, since you know that you will receive an inheritance from the Lord as a reward. It is the Lord Christ you are serving" (Col. 3:23-24, TNIV). Jacob has love and faith. But what about hope?

Hope Work

Jacob has not forgotten his destiny as a person of promise.[6] Jacob is part of a holy plan, engaged in a divine project, enlisted in God-

---

6. The promise is found in Genesis 15:1-5; 17:1-8; 22:17-18; 26:24; 27:27-29; 28:13-15.

work. He has seen the promise of family amply fulfilled in his eleven sons and daughters (the first part of the promise). But the land his family is to inherit remains unoccupied.

Several factors lead Jacob homeward. First, when his barren but beloved wife Rachel conceives and bears Joseph, Jacob now has a complete family and can fruitfully return to his homeland (30:25). A second factor is that Jacob has a dream (at approximately the same time) in which God says, "Now leave this land at once and go back to your native land" (31:13).

God has promised to be with Jacob at Bethel (28:15). Now once again God promises to be with Jacob but this time on condition that he return home (31:13). Jacob sees his work as part of God's grand plan to renew everything and to bring about his realm on earth. In the same way, work today can be hope work, not only because some of it can outlast this world, a subject to which we will turn later, but because it is part of God's long-term intention to renew people and all creation.

What makes work God-pleasing and God-blessed is not that God's name and Word are spoken out loud but that the work is done in love, faith, and hope. With these virtues (which are not human achievements but divine encouragements), even slave work can become holy work.[7]

For Discussion and Reflection

What does it mean for you to work with love, faith, and hope? Give some examples. What difference will it make to view your daily work as part of God's grand plan of renewing everything by bringing his rule into all of life and creation?

---

7. For a study on virtues see Iain Benson, "Virtues," in Robert Banks and R. Paul Stevens, eds., *The Complete Book of Everyday Christianity* (Downers Grove, Ill.: InterVarsity Press, 1997), pp. 1,069-72.

4

Vocational Work — Joseph

My object in living is to unite
My avocation and my vocation
As my two eyes make one in sight.

Robert Frost, "Two Tramps in Mud Time"

Unfortunately the word *vocation* is badly used today and, had I the power to do so, I would eliminate it entirely and replace it with the other translation of the original Latin word, *vocatio*, namely *calling*. While *vocation* has come to be identified with occupation, the word *calling* invites the question "Who?" Who is doing the calling? The most fundamental fact about calling and living vocationally is that we are first of all called to Someone before we are called to do something. That lesson is one Jacob is slowly learning, culminating in wisdom in his old age as he goes down to Egypt to be reunited with his son Joseph. Joseph himself is learning to live vocationally. It is something we desperately need and are in a process of losing.[1]

---

1. Much of this chapter was first published in R. Paul Stevens, *Down-to-Earth Spirituality: Encountering God in the Ordinary, Boring Stuff of Life* (Downers Grove, Ill.: InterVarsity Press, 2003), pp. 136-48. Permission granted.

The Spoiled Brat

Joseph's life is always of interest because of its dramatic turn of events — a real rags-to-riches story. But besides its dramatic quality, Joseph's story engages us at the level of living vocationally. At its simplest level, the story is about the eleventh son of Jacob who is the favored son, dressed in a richly ornamented robe so that he does not have to work, as do his brothers. They hate him because of his favored position, because of his dreams in which they are pictured bowing down to him, and also because he brought a bad report of them to their father (Gen. 37:2). So one day when Joseph goes out to the field to find out how things are going, they try to do away with him, first by throwing him into a dry cistern to die of malnutrition and thirst, and then by selling him to passing Midianite traders carrying spices to Egypt. The brothers, by the same kind of deceit that has passed from generation to generation, bring Joseph's special coat, now stained with animal blood, to Jacob and, without actually lying, invite him to draw his own conclusions: "We found this. Examine it to see whether it is your son's robe" (37:32). Jacob concludes that a wild animal has torn Joseph to shreds, when in fact it is his wild brothers who have torn him from the family. Jacob refuses to be comforted, because his life is bound up in the children of his favorite wife, Rachel, and with Joseph in particular.

Meanwhile Joseph ends up in Egypt, where he is sold as a slave to work in Potiphar's house. There, as everywhere else, Joseph rises into leadership and is placed in complete charge of the household. But when seduced by Mrs. Potiphar, he runs away, leaving only his coat behind. Falsely accused (through another deceptive piece of clothing), he lands up in another pit — a prison. There he interprets the dreams of Pharaoh's butler and baker, inserting his hopeful prophecy for the butler with the words, "Mention me to Pharaoh and get me out of this prison" (40:14). The butler forgets, at least for a long time, until Pharaoh himself has a disturbing dream and cannot get it interpreted by his wise men and magicians. Enter Joseph.

Joseph confesses, "I cannot do it, but God will give Pharaoh the answer he desires" (41:16). Many people imagine that God cannot be found in high-ranking political circles or in the board-rooms of multinational corporations. But Pharaoh himself says, "God has made all this known to you" (v. 39). Then, partly at Joseph's suggestion, Pharaoh hires Joseph to be second to him to garner food during the seven years of plenty for distribution during the upcoming seven years of famine. According to the dreams of Pharaoh, these are predicted.

If ever there were a prison to palace story, this is it! Joseph receives an Egyptian name (Zaphenath-Paneah), an Egyptian wife, a chariot, and almost unlimited power. In this role he saves the Egyptian nation and, as we shall see, saves even his own family. Joseph is a stunning example of a full-time servant of God in a so-called secular situation. Further, he performs "full-time ministry" without receiving a specific, personal call by God, yet he is truly living out his calling.

The plot thickens as the famine takes hold. Jacob sends Joseph's brothers to Egypt to buy grain. But Jacob, now with his favoritism transferred from Joseph to Benjamin, the one remaining son of Rachel, sends all except Benjamin down to get food "because he was afraid that harm might come to him" (42:4). The sons present themselves before Joseph and bow low. Joseph recognizes them but keeps his Egyptian disguise (one more pretense) and uses a translator as though he cannot understand what they are saying. Joseph realizes that his dreams are coming true. But he does not identify himself. Is he still struggling to forgive? Does he willfully hold back his identity because he needs to know whether his brothers have come to terms with what they have done to him? Does he wonder whether they have repented? He tries to find out by putting them through a simulation of his own dreadful experiences at their hands, accusing them of being spies (as he had "spied" for his father on them), throwing them in prison (as he had been cast into the pit in Dothan), and then releasing them on condition that Simeon stay behind as a hostage while the rest return to get the remaining brother, Benjamin.

Finally, after the passing of a long time, they persuade Jacob to let Benjamin, his one remaining son of Rachel, go to Egypt.

There follows a recognition scene that is one of the most moving in all literature. It is Judah who finally breaks Joseph down and achieves a reconciliation of the brothers. Then Joseph says, "It was not you who *sent* me here, but God" (45:8) and "It was to save lives that God *sent* me ahead of you" (v. 5).[2] In hindsight, Joseph recognizes his life as a vocational expression, although there had been early indications that God was leading him.

Three Roles

We have much to learn from Joseph about living vocationally. It is much more than having an occupation. First, Joseph has a *career*. For the first seventeen years of his life (from privilege to the pit), he follows in his father's steps as a shepherd "tending the flocks with his brothers" (37:2). A career is an occupation which one normally expects to undertake for a long period, possibly one's lifetime, though today people have four or five careers (with several assignments in each career) and have to keep reinventing themselves. Then Joseph gets a *job* (this is the period from the pit to prison), working as a slave in Potiphar's household. A job is work undertaken simply to survive. For much of the world today, people undertake work merely to survive with no sense that they are fulfilling a higher calling or doing work that fits their gifts and talents. But when Joseph is elevated from the prison to the palace, he discovers a *vocation,* a calling.

Vocation is much more than simply working. It is the summons of God to belong to him, to live God's way, and to do God's work in the world. I have been a pastor, a student worker, a carpenter, a businessperson, and a professor. But that is only part of my calling. I am also called to be a husband and father, a son and a grandfather, a friend, a citizen. I express my calling by living my whole life to God's glory. So Joseph, possibly more clearly toward the end, realizes that he was sent by God as a missionary to Egypt.

---

2. Italics mine. Significantly the Latin word for "sending" is *missio,* the word from which we get the English word "mission." Joseph has a mission from God.

36

This holy mission was to manage the resources of the land, not only for the Egyptians but also for the family of promise. Even slave work can get taken up into the calling of God and be given purpose.

Significantly, Joseph is a model management consultant. He gains a global view, defines the problem, recommends strategy, and undertakes to support the CEO (here represented by Pharaoh) in the process of implementation. In this case Joseph really "hired himself on," which was not crass selfish ambition but taking inspired entrepreneurial initiative. But Joseph was also an example of someone tempted in the area of his calling.

Three Temptations

The first of Joseph's temptations is to be the *architect of his own fulfillment.* As a young man, he has a dream in which his brothers all bow down to him. Given this amazing dream of greatness, he uses it to manipulate his brothers. One would think that, after their reaction to the first dream (eleven sheaves bowing down to his sheaf), Joseph would hold the next vision in his heart. But no, he blurts out the second one — the sun and moon (father and mother) and the eleven stars (his brothers) all bowing down to him. Added to this, Joseph is a tattletale (37:2), bringing a bad report of the brothers to Jacob. So they hate him the more. It seems that he is trying to *make* the vision happen. When we have a great vision, a mission that grips us, a "call" for our lives, it is always tempting to scheme about the dream without waiting for God, without depending for our next move on the God who creates and sustains us. Joseph has to learn this the hard way.

His second temptation is in the *sexual* area. He is seduced by Mrs. Potiphar, invited to go to bed with her. No one would know if he had done it, and a liaison with an important person could possibly stand him in good stead in the long run. But he courageously addresses both his own conscience and hers: he has a duty to his master ("My master has withheld nothing from me except you"). Then he calls a spade a spade: "How then could I do such a wicked thing and sin against God?" (39:9). This happens day after day until she catches him by the cloak. He escapes without his cloak, which she then uses as evidence against him, just as Joseph's brothers had before used his torn cloak as evidence of his death. Temptation in the sexual area thrives in the workplace, as do temptations to power and status. But this temptation needs to be named in the way Joseph did; he correctly called it a sin against God and his neighbor. Sometimes we can fight it directly; often, like Joseph, we must flee.

Joseph's third temptation is to locate his *identity* in his occupation. In Egypt, Pharaoh raises him from prison to the palace. Joseph has an Egyptian name, an Egyptian wife, Egyptian culture, and an all-consuming job. He is Mr. Second-in-Command. Many people have surnames derived from an ancestor's occupation — carter, smith, bolter, carpenter, carver, or weaver, for example. So becoming identified with one's occupation is understandable, though dangerous. It happens at parties. "What do you do?" For some, to answer that they are retired or unemployed implies having no identity at all. With great wisdom St. Augustine advised that if you want to find out who people are, don't ask them what they do but what they love.[3]

Regarding a career, it is easy to think we are the architects of our own fulfillment. In our jobs we can make moral compromises. We can also allow ourselves to be totally absorbed by the work dimensions, whereas calling is much, much more. But our daily work gets taken up in our calling. God has summoned us to participate in his grand plan of renewing everything and bringing shalom. Our work is part of this but only part.

For Discussion and Reflection

Which of the three work temptations Joseph faced is the one you most commonly encounter? How do you deal with it?

3. David Lyle Jeffrey, trans., "Introduction," in Walter Hilton, *Toward a Perfect Love* (Portland, Ore.: Multnomah Press, 1985), p. xxv.

What difference does it make to your work motivation and work ethic that your work is part of, though not all of, the call of God for your life?

What would it be like for you if, as Robert Frost proposes in the introductory quote to this chapter, your vocation and avocation (namely your hobbies, leisure activities, and non-work life) were all one?

5

Spirit Work — Bezalel

The Holy Spirit "speaks" and "helps." He never violates an individual, never attacks and destroys him, but rather brings the actual gifts and potentialities of a person to full development. We only become real people when the Holy Spirit takes up residence in us.

Arnold Bittlinger, *Gifts and Graces:*
A Commentary on 1 Corinthians 12–14

One dangerous yet widely spread belief today is that God gives his Spirit to people in the form of spiritual gifts solely for ministry in the church. But spiritual gifts are intended for all the people of God so that they can enter into God's beautiful work of transforming creation, culture, and people. And we learn from this that the most significant way in which God's spiritual gifts are demonstrated in the world is through our work.

Speaking to this theme in his seminal study, *Work in the Spirit*, Miroslav Volf says:

The Spirit is the giver of all life, and hence all work, as an expression of human life, draws its energy out of the fullness of the divine Spirit's energy. When human beings work, they work only because God's Spirit has given them power and talent to work. Without God's preserving and sustaining grace, no work would be possible.[1]

Volf approaches the role of the Spirit in work theologically, but unfortunately offers little textual support. However, it is not difficult to find New Testament passages that refer to spiritual gifts both for ministry within the church and for work in the world. For example, in Romans 12:3-8 Paul refers not only to the gift of prophesying, something that might occur mainly in a church context, but also to the gifts of serving, encouraging, giving, and leading — activities that could take place anywhere in the workplace. Furthermore, according to this passage, the "anointing" of the Spirit often seems to appear in the context of doing something practical such as serving or teaching. The person who gives shows the Spirit's anointing in the way that person gives — that is, with generosity — while in the case of the person who administers or leads, the leader's diligence demonstrates the Spirit's enabling (12:7-8). But even in the Old Testament we have a striking example of how the Spirit is active in work and the worker.

To explore this we turn to the only person in the Old Testament of whom it is said "he was filled with the Spirit of God." His name is Bezalel and he is my patron saint — a carpenter, an artisan, an artist, and a teacher — all aspects of daily work in my own life. This cryptic but wonderfully evocative Old Testament story prophetically anticipates what all believers are meant to be and do in the world now that the Spirit has been poured out on all.

Where Bezalel Fits in the Big Story

First, we must put this wonderful passage from Exodus 35 in the larger context of the story of the people of Israel. It is embedded in the story of Israel's Exodus from Egypt, that is, the departure of the descendants of Abraham, Isaac, and Jacob from slavery. This

---

1. Miroslav Volf, *Work in the Spirit: Toward a Theology of Work* (New York: Oxford University Press, 1991), p. 121.

second of the first five books has three high points. First comes the deliverance from enslavement — a mighty rescue by the outstretched hand of God. Next comes God's giving the covenant and the law at Mt. Sinai — the Ten Commandments, which stipulated the lifestyle of the people who belonged to God in a binding covenant. But the third high point — and this is where Bezalel and his helper Oholiab enter in — is building the tent or tabernacle where God would meet with the people. First there is salvation. (In years to come the Israelites would look back to the Exodus in the same way Christians look back to the cross and say, "There I was rescued.") This is followed by a wonderful commitment to live as a covenant people. But, thirdly and finally, there is the presence of God with his people, symbolized by the tent and the ark containing the tablets of the Ten Commandments and the cover for the place of atonement, along with the articles needed for making sacrifices, the altars, and the vestments worn by the priests.

Alan Coe, in his commentary on the book of Exodus, says, "If the law was a verbal expression of God's holiness, the Tent was a visible parable of it, and the nation of Israel was intended to be a walking illustration of it." To which he adds, "the entire aim of the construction of the Tent is so that God's presence may be experienced in the very midst of Israel."[2] Here, then, are some of the things we learn about the Spirit and work from this story:

Three Dimensions of Spirit-gifting for Work in the World

Moses says to the people that God "has filled [Bezalel] with the Spirit of God, with wisdom, with understanding, with knowledge, and with all kinds of skills — to make artistic designs for work in gold, silver, and bronze" (35:31-32, TNIV) — all for the purpose of making a sacred meeting place with God, the tent or tabernacle. Three dimensions of Spirit-gifting are represented in this account:

---

2. Alan Coe, *Exodus: An Introduction and Commentary* (Downers Grove, Ill.: InterVarsity, 1973), pp. 23, 39.

first, wisdom, which means practical intelligence and vision — seeing and designing and figuring out how to do it; second, understanding and knowledge, which give clarity in problem-solving; and third, skill, which is practical ability, hands and heart joined in doing.

God gives these gifts of the Spirit to his people in the workplace, uniquely to a few under the old covenant, but personally, universally, and permanently under the new covenant in Jesus. Later, in chapter 35 of Exodus, God says that he has given both Bezalel and Oholiab the ability to teach others how to work metal, fabrics, and wood, crafting beautiful things (v. 34). From this we see that the Spirit empowers people to show others how to do good and beautiful things in the world by passing on to them wisdom, understanding, and practical ability.

Three Components of Gift Discernment

How can we know whether we have been given our gifts by God and for God's purposes?

First, we can be directly appointed by God. God called Bezalel and Oholiab by name, selecting them to do a special, practical project for God. Similarly, we are called by God to serve him and his purposes in the church and the world. He calls us by name. Every one of us is called, not just pastors and missionaries. This is wonderful news. God calls us by name. "John, Sau-Yen, Sandra, José, come to me." We all have a vocation, a calling, which is much more than a career; it is the empowering summons of God to participate in his grand plan of renewing everything. A career is something we choose, something we push to succeed in. But a calling is something for which we are summoned. It's as if God has our telephone number and he keeps redialing until we answer.

Second, God himself can stir our hearts to do the work. The Hebrew word used here means literally that their hearts were lifted up to become involved in this work (36:2). The Spirit moves us inwardly to want to do the work God has called us to. Assuming that it can't be God's will if we *want* to do a particular thing is a sad distortion of the Christian faith. Just the reverse is often the case. If we have the mind of Christ, if God's Spirit is in us and we are immersed in the realm of the Spirit, usually what we want to do *is* the will of God. God stirs our hearts. To help us recognize the deep stirrings of the heart, we can ask questions like these: When we are engaged in certain activities, do we lose all sense of time? What do we daydream about? What kind of things, even from childhood onward, have we enjoyed and felt we did successfully?

Speaking to the meaning of calling, Frederick Buechner explains that when we are searching for the right vocation, it is important to listen to the right voice:

> [The word "vocation"] comes from the Latin *vocare*, to call, and means the work a [person] is called to by God. There are all different kinds of voices calling you to all different kinds of work, and the problem is to find out which is the voice of God rather than of Society, say, or the Super-ego, or Self-Interest.
>
> Neither the hair shirt nor the soft berth will do. The place God calls you to is the place where your deep gladness and the world's deep hunger meet.[3]

Third, our gifts and callings need to be recognized by others. In the Exodus account Moses, as a representative of the people, selects and appoints those whom God has himself appointed: "Moses summoned Bezalel and Oholiab and every skilled person to whom the LORD had given ability and who was willing to come and do the work" (36:2). Calling can be confirmed by those closest to us — family members, church leaders, and friends and colleagues. What a powerful thing to be able to say to someone, "I think you are unusually gifted and qualified to do such and such." Parents especially can help their children in this way; in fact, the Puritans emphasized that one of a parent's responsibilities is to help children discover their personal callings.

---

3. Frederick Buechner, *Wishful Thinking: A Seeker's ABC* (San Francisco: HarperSanFrancisco, 1993), p. 119.

Three Outcomes of Doing the Work of God's Spirit

When we do the work to which God's Spirit calls us, we see the following results:

First, our work glorifies God. Bringing honor to God can be our deepest motivation for work in the world, whether in business, the trades, homemaking, government service, health care, education, art and entertainment, communication, advertising, or any other area. Indeed, as the biblical story unfolds we see that Bezalel and Oholiab are partners with God in a divine-human enterprise, a partnership that in Paul's letter to the Corinthians is described as being "co-workers in God's service" (1 Cor. 3:9). When we design, maintain, and help, as well as fix and point to the meaning of things, we do the Lord's work. That is to say, when we embrace the rich and varied potential of creation — and not just when we preach sermons — we bring honor to God. Elsewhere in the New Testament Paul says that even slaves are serving and glorifying God. Twice he makes the point that our work is done primarily for Christ (Col. 3:22-24).

Second, our work is a practical way of loving our neighbors. Obviously Bezalel and Oholiab were serving their neighbors — creating a place for them to worship God. It may not be as obvious that people who work in service industries or maintenance roles, such as garbage collectors and air traffic controllers, are also serving their neighbors. But in fact they are, whether directly or indirectly. Arnold Bittlinger notes:

> In exercising spiritual gifts we are involved in the restoration (the bringing together again) of God's perfect work in creation. An activity can only be characterized as a spiritual gift when it assists in the restoration of creation, and contributes towards the healing of a sick world. But it will also be true that every such activity and contribution is a gift of the Spirit, even when the individual involved is unconscious of it.[4]

4. Arnold Bittlinger, *Gifts and Graces: A Commentary on 1 Corinthians 12–14* (Grand Rapids: Eerdmans, 1967), p. 25.

Third, our work embellishes human life and creates beauty. In Exodus 28:2 God tells Moses to have sacred garments made for Aaron "to give him dignity and honor." On the first night of one of my Everyday Spirituality classes, as students were introducing themselves, one woman said, "I am *just* a hairdresser." At the end of the course she had a different perspective on herself and her role in the world: now she said, "I make people beautiful, and I do a lot of counseling."

We can create beauty not just in music and the visual arts, but also in a meal or a deal, a voice or an invoice, an operation or a co-operation, a community formed or an immunity created, a test or a quest, a swept floor or a forgiven heart, a canvas painting or a computer program, a plaything or a work-thing, a toy or a tool.

Is the Spirit's presence just for the Church to sing spiritual songs and to worship and to build other Christians up? No. The Holy Spirit empowers us to do good and beautiful things in the world. Therefore we should pray to be filled with the Spirit to do whatever we do better, more heartily, and with all our might, like Bezalel, Oholiab, and the other workers with them. For it is the Lord Christ we are serving, and it is our neighbor we are loving (whether directly or indirectly). All of this can be something beautiful for God.

For Discussion and Reflection

What evidence have you seen of the presence of the Spirit in the work done by your colleagues? In your own work?

How might the Spirit be working in people who do not regard themselves as belonging to God or who are not otherwise actively seeking the Spirit?

The First Five Books: A Brief Summary

What do we learn from the first five books of the Bible?

First, work is part of our God-imaging dignity. We are made to work. Work is mandated by God and is both intrinsically good (good in itself) and extrinsically good (good for what it produces).

Second, work has been corrupted and degraded by human sin, as seen in Genesis chapter 3. This has led to predatory competition, blaming, toiling, and frustration, symbolized by "thorns, thistles and sweat."

Third, work is to be undertaken with integrity and justice. This includes caring for creation, paying wages promptly, offering reasonable credit to others, and providing for the poor (Deut. 15–25).

Fourth, work is limited by Sabbath (Exod. 20:8; Deut. 5:12). Work is not good if it is all-consuming, permitting no rest and reflection.[1]

Finally, work can be virtuous when undertaken with faith, hope, and love and is an expression of God's call for all human beings. Thankfully, it is the Holy Spirit — and not we ourselves — who brings creativity and beauty to our daily work.

---

1. An exposition of rest and Sabbath can be found in R. Paul Stevens, "A Day of Rest" (chapters 19–21) in *Seven Days of Faith: Every Day Alive with God* (Colorado Springs: Navpress, 2001).

PART TWO

Stewardship Work

An Introduction to the Historical Books

For the Hebrews there simply was no secular history. None. Everything that happened, happened in a world penetrated by God. Since they did not talk a lot about God in their storytelling, it is easy to forget that God is always the invisible and mostly silent presence in everything that is taking place.

Eugene Peterson, *The Message*

The first five books of the Bible, also called the Pentateuch, introduced us to the intrinsic and extrinsic value of work. As we trace the stories of workers in the next section of the Bible, usually called the Historical Books — from Joshua to Esther — the main theme is how God raises up leaders to help God's people reach maturity and their final destination. In the language of biblical theology, that "final destination" is a realm that is both here and now, concretely expressed in the world, and, at the same time, not yet fully come and beyond even this present creation. In this section we learn a great deal about a particular kind of work, namely the labor of leadership.

Judges, Kings, and Little People with Influence

This section of the canon begins with the people entering the promised land, not with Moses at the head but with Moses' disciple, Joshua. When the people first settled into their homeland, they were essentially a tribal confederacy headed by God. God was their sovereign. The nation was to be a true theocracy with God as the central authority and governing head of the tribes. In this context, God appointed certain people as judges. These were not jurists who presided in courts, as we might use the term "judges" today. They were inspired leaders chosen by God to deliver the people in crisis situations. The long list of these judges includes such superb examples as Samuel, who never took a salary from the people, as well as such unsavory characters as Samson, whom God used, in spite of his sexual addiction, to deliver the people. Among the events that took place during the time of the judges is the story of a foreign woman who embraced the family of God and showed tremendous leadership in her own life — namely, Ruth. In the next chapter we will explore her story as an example of survival work. This is especially relevant because millions of people in the world today do not enjoy fulfilling and talent-expressing work but struggle through their chores merely to survive.

But before we begin, we need to remember that at the time of the judges the people were enamored with models of hierarchical leadership practiced in the surrounding nations with the result that God's people, too, demanded a human sovereign. Just as people in the Pentateuch had asked Moses to speak to God on their behalf and act as a mediator, so people now were not satisfied to have an invisible heavenly Ruler but wanted a human representative as leader. "Appoint a king to lead us, such as all the other nations have," they said (1 Sam. 8:5). Reluctantly, it seems, God granted their wish and gave them in turn Saul, David, and Solomon. But because of Solomon's oppressive rule, a civil war broke out, followed by a division of the nation into two parts and a succession of, for the most part, truly bad leaders. Ultimately, God's displeasure with the leaders and people led to the northern kingdom being taken into captivity to Assyria, the local superpower; a century and a half later the southern kingdom, Judah, was taken captive by Babylonia, the new superpower. In these situations God spoke, largely through prophets, to explain why things turned out so badly. Why had things turned out this way? Because of the people's sin. But the fault lay not only with the common people. Many of the leaders contributed to the problem, even some of the good leaders.

What Leaders Do

The stories in this section of the Bible show examples of the work that both good and bad leaders do. We see good leaders building a community and a nation, standing for righteousness, championing the poor and marginalized, being stewards of the talents and gifts of the people, empowering the people, and pointing the people in the ultimate direction in which they should be moving. All these are characteristics of good leaders, whether they are people of faith or not. But in the context of the people of God, leaders have one more obligation: to depend on God themselves and to create in the people a desire to depend not primarily on the human leader but on God. As we shall see, David, Esther, and Nehemiah all did this magnificently.

But for an example of a bad leader, consider the tragic case of Solomon, who though touted for his wisdom and grand building schemes, proved in the end to be a bad leader. Reflecting on this, the Canadian business consultant John Dalla Costa says,

[The] Israelites' kings reverted to the tyrannies of power and ambition. Saul stopped listening to the wisdom of the prophets and succumbed to hubris. David slipped into idolatry for the love of a woman. Solomon, whose reputation for being wise turns out to be a millennia-old spin, squandered the nation's treasure and imposed servitude on his free people to build grand royal structures. Of course they had some redeeming qualities. Israel's anointed rulers did model worthy aspects of kingship: the warrior fierce and resolute in moral causes; the poet who conjures symbols and frames meaning; and the builder who creates the infrastructure for work and worship. But the prototype was incomplete and finally only fully defined by Jesus Christ. With the inscription "King of the Jews" nailed to his cross, Jesus exemplifies power emptied out to liberate others from suffering and enslavement.[1]

However, reading through Joshua, Judges, 1 and 2 Samuel, 1 and 2 Kings, 1 and 2 Chronicles, Esther, Nehemiah, and Ezra raises a particularly challenging question: While it is patently obvious why the "bad" kings fell — because of immorality, idolatry, and compromise, as well as adopting pagan practices such as offering their children in fire to the gods — why is it that the *good* kings, such as David and Solomon, also fell? Did they have a Shakespearean fatal flaw in their characters? In the case of David and Solomon it appears to have been their addiction to sex. But in spite of these tragic flaws, their story has a dimension that changes it from a saga of mistakes to the history of a people working in history towards a worthwhile and wonderful end. That is, in spite of the personal disasters of many people during this time of history, we can also discern in their actions what God was doing through it all.

What God Was Doing

God was at work. Israel was called not only to be a people that belonged to God in a covenant embodied in the formula, "I am your God and you are my people," like the marriage vow, but the people were also to be a concrete expression of the realm of God, God's dynamic and life-giving rule on earth. In this way Israel was to be a working model of God's sovereignty, an advance prototype, and a foretaste of something in the future. And in doing this Israel was to be a light to the other nations, winsomely attracting them to the worship of the only true God, as the prophet Zechariah foretold (Zech. 8:23). So *the way* people worked was a central dimen-

---

1. John Dalla Costa, *Magnificence at Work: Living Faith in Business* (Ottawa: Novalis, 2005), pp. 328-29. A passage in Ezek. 21:27 reinforces Dalla Costa's point: "The crown will not be restored until he to whom it rightfully belongs shall come; to him I will give it" (TNIV).

sion of this vision. It was not merely a spiritual realm concerned with right worship, prayer, and liturgical correctness. It was about everyday life. And that is true about the rest of the big story as well.[2]

In Part Two we will consider several individual stories of important leaders. We begin with the story of Ruth the Moabite who became the grandmother of David, king of Israel, and an ancestor of Jesus. Then we look at David, who became king of Israel and united the nation under his God-fearing leadership. Esther, a Jew, was providentially made queen in pagan Persia when God's people were later taken into exile. And Nehemiah was cupbearer to the Persian king and a shrewd leader when that king allowed some of the Jews to return to their homeland to rebuild the wall and the temple, thus preparing the way for the coming of the Messiah. We will see that the so-called Historical Books provide us with a vision that embodies the prayer Jesus taught, "Your kingdom come . . . on earth as it is in heaven" (Matt. 6:10).

2. See Amos 9:13, Mic. 4:3ff., Isa. 11:1-9, and Hos. 2:18-23.

6

Survival Work — Ruth

Glaube an Christus und tue, was du schuldig bist zu tun in deinem Berufe. (Believe in Christ and do whatever needs to be done in your profession.)

Martin Luther

People in the western and northern hemispheres are busily trying to bring soul back into the workplace and developing their right brains to keep a creative advantage over the developing world, to which manufacturing has largely been transferred. Meanwhile, much of the rest of the world merely works to survive. And what is the meaning of that kind of work? Unfortunately, work for millions of people is not for self-realization and the expression of talent. For them work becomes merely a means of putting bread or rice on the table.

Perhaps no story in the Bible speaks to this situation more eloquently than the story of Ruth, the Moabite. It might be tempting to call this story "How to find a husband when none of the men around seems to be taking initiative" or "Never underestimate the advice given by your mother-in-law!" But this is a story of economic migration at a time of famine, and a story of return to the homeland to hunt for whatever work would help mother-in-law Naomi and daughter-in-law Ruth to survive. At this time, the only work available was gleaning, that is, picking up the leftovers after harvesters have taken off the best crop — a gracious provision of Scripture for the poor. It is also a story of romance, a story of a woman taking initiative to find a husband, a story of a great reversal in fortune, a story about foreign workers and forced migration. Above all, it is a story of how God is at work, even in survival work.

Three Widows Eking Out an Existence

Two Hebrews, Naomi and her husband Elimelech, and their two sons migrated from Bethlehem to Moab, a nearby pagan nation, in a time of famine. The sons married local women. Then tragedy struck — three times in fact. All three of the men in the family died, leaving three widows in the same house. When Naomi heard that rains had returned to Israel, she determined to return to her homeland alone, advising her two daughters-in-law to find husbands among their own people. Orpah, Ruth's sister, remained in Moab, but Ruth determined to stay with Naomi in covenant love, uttering the famous words: "Where you go I will go, and where you stay I will stay. Your people will be my people and your God my God. Where you die I will die, and there I will be buried" (Ruth 1:16-17). So they migrated back to Naomi's homeland, where Ruth provided for her mother-in-law by gleaning in the field during the barley harvest. In effect, Ruth is the Old Testament Dumpster-diver, living off people's leftovers.

As it turned out, providentially, she gleaned in the field of Boaz, a relative of Naomi, someone who actually was a family guardian or kinsman-redeemer, a person who had the power and responsibility to redeem a relative from slavery or to restore family land that had been mortgaged. At this point Naomi, the great matchmaker, recognized that Boaz was showing interest in Ruth and cleverly arranged for Ruth, decked out in her best finery and dabbed with perfume, to indicate she wanted Boaz as her husband. She did this in a culturally accepted manner during the night when Boaz was sleeping at the edge of the grain pile, placing herself at his feet. "Spread the corner of your garment over me," she said to Boaz when he woke and found her at his feet (3:9). Boaz got the message and determined that unless a nearer relative exercised his option to buy the land and marry Ruth — since both were tied together in Israelite law — he would take Ruth as his wife. And so it turned out that Ruth, a foreigner, became the grandmother of King David and an ancestor of Jesus. This shows once again God's amazing way of including all people to accomplish his wonderful purpose of transforming the world and humanity. It is a grand story: a widowed woman finds a loving husband; a bitter mother becomes joyful; tragedy is turned into good fortune. But now the question is, Where do we find God active in all this survival work?

First, God is involved in the provision of work itself. Work is a good gift of God. It is also a way of providing for oneself and one's family. But in those cases where, through systemic unemployment, through no fault of the would-be worker, no remunerated employment is available, there is always unpaid work that can be done. Even the search for work is work. Good work. But more than that, threaded through this story is the *providence* of God. It is no accident that Ruth gleaned in the field of a kinsman-redeemer. Similarly, our lives are not bundles of accidents. God is working out a good purpose through all the events and circumstances of our lives, even the most difficult ones, even mistakes.

Second, God is also active in our relationship with coworkers and bosses, as Ruth discovered with Boaz. All people bear the image of God, reflecting something of the dignity and character of God, however twisted and distorted their own lives may be. And sometimes God is involved in *personal speech* when someone is able to utter God's name and purpose in words like, "The Lord be with you," or "The Lord bless you," or in the beautiful words that Boaz spoke to Ruth, "May you be richly rewarded by the Lord, the God of Israel, under whose wings you have come to take refuge" (2:12).

Third, God is predisposed to provide for the poor and is especially present in the care of the poor and needy. This is reflected in the gleaning legislation of the Old Testament, in the passion of the prophets, and, not least, in the ministry of Jesus. The Old Testament had a welfare system suited to an agrarian society. But today we need an even broader and more diverse strategy for charitable giving. The great medieval Jewish philosopher, Maimonides (Moses ben Maimon, 1135-1204), defined the eight levels of charity this way:

1. A person gives, but only when asked by the poor.
2. A person gives, but is glum when giving.
3. A person gives cheerfully, but less than he or she should.
4. A person gives without being asked, but gives directly to the poor. Now the poor know who gave them help and the giver, too, knows whom he or she has benefited.
5. A person throws money into the house of someone who is poor. The poor person does not know to whom he or she is indebted, but the donor knows whom he or she has helped.
6. A person gives a donation in a certain place and then turns away so that he or she does not know which of the poor has been helped, but the poor person knows to whom he or she is indebted.
7. A person gives anonymously to a fund for the poor. Here the poor do not know to whom they are indebted, and the donor does not know who has been helped.

But the highest form of giving is this:

8. Money is given to prevent another person from becoming poor, such as providing a job, teaching a trade, or setting up a person in business so as to spare that person the dreadful alternative of holding out a hand for charity. This is the highest step and the summit of charity's golden ladder.[1]

This last and highest form of charity points the way to one of the best hopes of the poor today in the majority world: micro and mid-sized economic development through organizations like Nadácia Integra, World Vision, and Opportunities International that lend money to people in need to enable them to start a business.

1. Cited in William E. Diehl and Judith Ruhe Diehl, *It Ain't Over Till It's Over* (Minneapolis: Augsburg Books, 2003), pp. 129-30.

So survival work is good work, no matter how routine or menial it may be.[2] It is godly work. It is work in which God is present. It is work that one can do for the love of one's family and neighbor. And almost all survival work engages people fully — mind, body, and soul — and can be done, as Paul instructed the slaves in Colossae, for the Lord.

For Discussion and Reflection

Consider and discuss the implications and challenges of the following words of Martin Luther: "A shoemaker, a smith, a farmer, each has his manual occupation and work; and yet, at the same time, all are eligible to act as priests and bishops. Every one of them in his occupation or handicraft ought to be useful to his fellows, and serve them in such a way that the various trades are all directed to the best advantage of the community, and promote the well-being of body and soul, just as the organs of the body serve each other."[3]

2. A good resource for chores and survival work is that of Robert Banks, "Chores," in Robert Banks and R. Paul Stevens, eds., *The Complete Book of Everyday Christianity* (Downers Grove, Ill.: InterVarsity Press, 1997), pp. 107-9. Other resources on chores are D. Adam, *The Edge of Glory: Modern Prayers in the Celtic Tradition* (London: Triangle/SPCK, 1985); E. Dreyer, *Earth Crammed with Heaven: A Spirituality of Everyday Life* (New York: Paulist, 1994); C. Forbes, *Catching Sight of God: The Wonder of Everyday* (Portland, Ore.: Multnomah, 1987); Brother Lawrence, *The Practice of the Presence of God* (Albion Park, Pa.: Hadidian, 1989); K. A. Rabuzzi, *The Sacred and the Feminine: Toward a Theology of Housework* (New York: Seabury, 1982).

3. Cited by Cyril Eastwood, *The Priesthood of All Believers: An Examination of the Doctrine from the Reformation to the Present Day* (Minneapolis: Augsburg Publishing House, 1962), p. 12.

7

Royal Work — David

No two people have exactly the same calling. That is why we need to mull over many examples if we are trying to apply them to ourselves. None will ever quite fit; some may suggest useful clues, and some may leave us cold.

Michael Novak, *Business as a Calling:*
Work and the Examined Life

One day as I was dumping wheelbarrows full of drain rock around a newly poured concrete foundation, I turned to my friend, whose house we were building, and said, "What will become of me?" It was a low moment in my construction-work experience. He replied, "Never forget, Moses had two useless careers, first as an administrator in Egypt and then as a shepherd in Midian. But God redeemed those useless careers to make him a shepherd and administrator of the people of God." Make no mistake about it: nothing is wasted in our lives.

Nothing was wasted in David's life, either. We know more about David than almost any other character in the Bible, beginning with his early days as a shepherd and his anointing by Samuel as future king, then his service in King Saul's court as a musician to soothe Saul's frayed nerves, his exile while Saul hunted him down, his emergence as king, his military conquests to secure the nation, his complicated and dysfunctional family life, and his final days when, as an old man, he got his feet warmed in bed and appointed his son Solomon as his successor. His story covers large portions of the books of Samuel, Kings, and Chronicles, quite apart from what we can learn about his life from the book of Psalms. For the most part, David did two kinds of work, in the military and the political spheres, but his experience as a shepherd prepared him to do both. Sometimes, as in the case of David, we can see clues about our giftedness, capacities, and inclinations from earliest childhood.

The Soldier and the Politician

David learned how to lead as a shepherd, which prepared him for politics, and he learned how to overcome threats and opposition while caring for sheep, which prepared him for a military career. David told King Saul how his shepherd's work had prepared him for military service when he offered to confront the giant Goliath saying, "Your servant has been keeping his father's sheep. When a lion or a bear came and carried off a sheep from the flock, I went after it, struck it, and rescued the sheep from its mouth. When it turned on me, I seized it by its hair, struck it and killed it. Your servant has killed both the lion and the bear" (1 Sam. 17:34-36).

David's military career occupies a large part of the biblical record. He was a consummate soldier, overcoming the Philistine threat many times, hiring himself out for a period as a mercenary, and then, as king, overcoming the factions and opponents that would threaten the emerging nation of Israel.

Is being in the military good work? Is being a politician good work? Christians have often argued over the merits of these two arenas of human enterprise and some in the first-century church argued that one could serve in the army only if one did not kill. But that seems to be a contradiction in terms. Many today do not see the military work as a Christian option, while others see it as legitimate work. Luther dealt with this in terms of his famous "two kingdoms" teaching, namely that in the kingdom of God one would not kill, but as we also live in the kingdom of this world we may actually be called to exercise justice as a soldier or even as an executioner.

Politics is certainly a complicated arena in which to serve God, laced as it so commonly is with intrigue, compromises, and under-the-table deals. But in spite of the difficulties of serving in both politics and the military, such service can be good work that actually benefits many people, whether one works in the military by providing security, or one labors in government, providing a community infrastructure in which people can thrive. David did both with zeal and excellence. In fact, the story of David not only describes these two kinds of human work but also gives us some important clues about how to carry out such work in a God-honoring and life-affirming way.

A Model Political Leader

As a political leader David provides a model that is almost without comparison. He had charisma. But he had something more — integrity. And "followership," without which there is no leadership, results from exercising integrity in all areas of life. Thus David was able to take a rag-tag group of rebels and discontents and shape them into a formidable army. He evoked so much loyalty that on one occasion when surrounded by enemies, three of his men risked their lives just to get a cup of water from his favorite well in Bethlehem — water that he promptly poured out on the ground when he realized the sacrifice involved in getting it.

Saul was obsessed with the threat that David represented to his own position. With an equally magnificent obsession to forgive, David refused to advance his own interests against his enemy, sparing Saul more than once when he easily could have eliminated him. And when Saul was finally killed in battle, David lamented the loss of the person God had anointed for that governing position. Thus David brilliantly combined his military career with his political career and became the second king of Israel. He was a king *par excellence,* a person who had a heart after God's own heart (Acts 13:22) and became a "herald of the coming kingdom of God," as Philip Greenslade put it.[1] To be a king like David was the highest of compliments (Ezek. 34:20-24).

Doing Royal Work after God's Own Heart

The ultimate meaning of David's life and work is aptly summed up by Paul in his sermon in Pisidian Antioch: David had "served God's purpose in his own generation" (Acts 13:36). That is what good sovereigns do. They rule and they serve. What can this mean to the ordinary work most of us do in offices, homes, community centers, schools, universities, and churches? In comparison to David's, our work may not seem significant. But we must not become discouraged. The fact is that most of us are doing royal work without even realizing it. Eugene Peterson says, "All true work combines these two elements of serving and ruling. Ruling is what we do; serving is the way we do it."[2]

How do royal leaders do their work "after God's own heart"?

First, royal leaders continue to do the right thing. As Paul said in his sermon, God found in David a person with a heart after his own heart, someone who would do "everything I want him to do" (Acts 13:22). David referred everything to God, consulted God, prayed to God as a matter of daily instinct, had a God-soaked life, and wanted the presence and pleasure of God more than anything. People in leadership, like good rulers, want to do the will of God not because it is always expedient but because it is right (1 Kings 9:4).

Second, royal leaders are motivated most deeply by the fear of God (2 Sam. 23:3). The fear of God is not sheer fright before a transcendent God but reverent awe. It has both a rational dimension — leading to ethical action — and an emotional dimension — leading to awe and loving intimacy. This is apparent in the

---

1. Philip Greenslade, *Leadership, Greatness, and Servanthood* (Minneapolis: Bethany, 1984), p. 57.

2. Eugene Peterson, *Leap Over a Wall: Earthly Spirituality for Everyday Christians* (San Francisco: HarperSanFrancisco, 1997), p. 33. Peterson's book is the finest there is on leadership and the story of David.

Psalms, where David pours out his heart to the Lord, sometimes thanking, sometimes expressing his anxiety and troubles, and sometimes appealing to God for help. For David, fear of God certainly did not mean bottling up emotions and hiding from him. Just the reverse. It meant exposing himself in humility to God's sovereign oversight.

Third, royal leaders are willing to receive advice and help. The extraordinary friendship of David and Jonathan is a case in point. It was no easy relationship because Jonathan, as Saul's son, was destined for the throne, so a relationship with David, Saul's rival, would prejudice Jonathan's chances. But he consistently defended David to his father and, more significantly, found ways of empowering him. Eugene Peterson comments with keen insight on this relationship: "Without Jonathan, David was at risk of either abandoning his vocation and returning to the simple life of tending sheep or developing a murderous spirit of retaliation to get even with the man who was despising the best that was within him."[3] When David was besieged and hunted like a dog by the insanely jealous Saul, Jonathan went out to David in the desert of Ziph "and helped him find strength in God" (1 Sam. 23:16). It is noteworthy that Jonathan did not tell David to rely on his friend but to find strength in God, something marvelously illustrated in the psalms attributed to David. The same point is made in 1 Samuel 30:6: when his followers were about to stone him, David again "found strength in the Lord his God."

Fourth, royal leaders are willing to face up to their faults. Michael Novak says, "We belong to the only moral majority there is: sinners."[4] No one is flawless. David was far from perfect. In fact, he had, like all the good kings in the Old Testament, a fatal flaw that compromised his stunning career. But it isn't just David or other good rulers who have a tragic flaw. To some degree we all have one, as Carlo Carretto discovered when writing from his experience in the solitude of the North African desert:

3. Peterson, *Leap Over a Wall,* p. 54.

4. Michael Novak, *Business as a Calling: Work and the Examined Life* (New York: The Free Press, 1996), p. 51.

In the depths lodges the most crucial fault, greater than any other even though it is hidden. It rarely, or perhaps never, breaks out in single concrete actions pushing towards the surface of the world. But from the depths, from the inmost layers of our being, it soaks in a poison which causes extreme damage. . . . Because it is hidden, or rather camouflaged, we can barely catch sight of it, and often only after a long time; but it is alive enough in our consciousness to be able to contaminate us and it weighs us down considerably more than the things which we habitually confess.[5]

David's list of flaws included numbering the people and having a sexual affair with Bathsheba (2 Sam. 11–12). David had a complicated history with the other sex. Abigail, another of his wives, represented beauty to him, and her double-edged beauty of character and countenance "recovered the beauty of the Lord for [David]. Abigail on her knees put David back on his knees," says Eugene Peterson.[6] But another beautiful woman, Bathsheba, became the means of David compromising his integrity. David's great gift of passion and heart had a shadow side — a weakness for sensuality. In fact, by having an affair with Bathsheba he committed three sins: adultery, murder, and lying.

But when the prophet Nathan confronted him with his sin in lusting after Bathsheba and murdering her husband to get her, David said, "I am the man." A phrase derived from the Latin, *felix culpa,* or "O happy sin," suggests the hope, even the good news, implicit in recognizing our sin, as David did. Much of religion purports to provide sin-management. But the true Good News is neither the art of sin-avoidance nor sin-management but forgiveness and new life.

Critical to giving leadership with integrity is knowledge of oneself. Almost all spiritual directors through the ages have recognized the interdependence of knowing God and knowing our-

5. Carlo Carretto, *Letters from the Desert,* trans. Rose Mary Hancock (Maryknoll, N.Y.: Orbis Books, 1972, 2002), pp. 61-62.

6. Peterson, *Leap Over a Wall,* p. 88.

selves. Catherine of Siena, one of the doctors of the church, speaking for God as she does in her *Dialogues,* says, "You cannot arrive at virtue except through knowing yourself and knowing me. And this knowledge is more perfectly gained in time of temptation, because then you know that you are nothing, since you have no power to relieve yourself of the sufferings and troubles you would like to escape."[7] And by self-knowledge, spiritual directors like Catherine of Siena do not mean, as modern and postmodern people might think today, self-actualization and a good, positive self-esteem. They mean knowing how needy we are. Without this we cannot know God fully. And we come to know ourselves, not so much on prayer retreats and immersions in the monastery, but in daily life, especially in our work. Ask David.

For Discussion and Reflection

Consider and respond to the following quote of Cardinal Wyszynski, mentor to the late Pope John Paul II: "Without external work we could not know ourselves fully, for only in daily work do we have a perfect opportunity to observe ourselves; it is then indeed that we discover the good and evil in ourselves, and we see our merits and our faults. . . . This work by the sweat of our brow lays bare the image of our soul and unveils its real expression."[8]

---

7. Catherine of Siena, *The Dialogues,* trans. Suzanne Noffke, OP, The Classics of Western Spirituality (New York: Paulist Press, 1980), p. 88.

8. Stefan Cardinal Wyszynski, *All You Who Labor: Work and the Sanctification of Daily Life* (Manchester, N.H.: Sophia Institute Press, 1995), p. 113.

8

Shrewd Work — Nehemiah

Up to the time of the Renaissance, people perceived the future little more than a matter of luck or the result of random variations, and most of their decisions were driven by instinct. . . . As Christianity spread across the western world, the will of a single God emerged as the orienting guide to the future. . . . The Renaissance and the Protestant Reformation would set the scene for the mastery of risk.

Peter L. Bernstein, *Against the Gods:*
The Remarkable Story of Risk

Jesus said something supremely relevant for the workplace, especially the commercial one: "Be as shrewd as snakes and as innocent as doves" (Matt. 10:16). Shrewdness in this context means being resourceful, clever, astute, and marked by a strong dose of practical wisdom. It is something exemplified in an extraordinary Old Testament person after whom a whole book is named. Nehemiah was a "shrewd" servant leader, in the best sense of that word. But as Robert Greenleaf notes in his groundbreaking study on leadership, *Servant Leadership: A Journey into the Nature of Legitimate Power and Greatness,* people who have been great role models of leadership were first of all servants and through their service to people became leaders. Biblical servant leadership takes this a step further, as we shall see. Biblical servant-leaders are first of all servants of God and then leaders and servants of people. But the call to be "shrewd," that is, to use wise, practical insight, takes the biblical understanding of servant leadership even further.[1]

Nehemiah, the Shrewd Leader

Nehemiah was a servant and a leader — servant to King Artaxerxes in Persia and eventually a leader of the scattered Jews returning to Jerusalem from exile to rebuild the city wall. But he was a servant-leader with a difference. His position in the royal court was to serve as cupbearer to the king. This means that he had one of the most trusted positions of service in the kingdom. In those days one popular way to assassinate a king was by poisoning his food or drink, so the cupbearer was charged to taste everything first. Here is a pagan king trusting a believer in Yahweh with his life. In this respect Nehemiah was like Joseph, Daniel, Esther, and Mordecai, worshipers of Yahweh who were placed in extraordinary positions of trust by pagan rulers.

As a pious Jew, strategically and providentially placed in the king's court, Nehemiah had two bosses, the Persian king and the King of kings. As the story unfolds, we discover that leadership is a form of work. It involves the purposeful expenditure of energy, demonstrating stewardship of human and material resources, inspiring others with a vision and mission, and showing appreciation of and empowering others. That's what leaders do. But, as we noted above, biblical servant leadership takes this a step further. It involves, first of all, being servants of God, and that makes an enormous difference. We might call this a two-pronged form of

---

1. Although the NIV and TNIV use the word "shrewd" in a contextual translation of Matt. 10:16, the Greek word *phronimos* otherwise has the general idea of "understanding associated with insight and wisdom, *sensible, thoughtful, prudent, wise*" (W. F. Arndt and F. W. Gingrich, *A Greek-English Lexicon of the New Testament and Other Early Christian Literature* [Chicago: The University of Chicago Press, 1952], p. 874). When not applied to snakes, therefore, these are the positive qualities of shrewdness that we refer to in this chapter.

servant leadership: serving people and their needs and serving God's purposes — and doing both at the same time! To do this well, leaders need to be shrewd and discriminating since there are always multiple possibilities and choices to be negotiated in order to realize maximum benefit for the good of the greatest number. It is possible to be shrewd and innocent at the same time, in other words, largely free of unmixed motives and innocent about evil (Rom. 16:19) and yet resourceful.

Briefly, the story goes like this. Nehemiah, in far-off Persia, almost five centuries before Christ, heard news of the terrible situation of the returned exiles living in the beloved city of Jerusalem with its walls in ruins. His instinct was to pray. But the king, noticing his sad face, asked for the cause and then posed the critical question: "What is it you want?" (Neh. 2:4). So Nehemiah shot a prayer to God, the famous "arrow prayer," requested permission to return to his native Jerusalem and to be given resources to rebuild the wall — a great example of a shrewd leader seizing the opportunity.

Nehemiah demonstrated extraordinary qualities of leadership. First, he scouted out the possibilities for rebuilding by secretly riding around the ruins of the wall before addressing the people with the challenge; then he got the people to work on the parts of the wall closest to their own homes. We also see him dealing shrewdly with opposition and responding effectively to the many challenges of a huge project. From this we can learn that if we have any passion for our work, any all-embracing purpose for our lives, there will be trouble. Nehemiah's great word to his opponents trying to seduce him to a private and dangerous meeting was, "I am carrying on a great project and cannot go down" (Neh. 6:3). His response invites an important question for all workers today: What is the great project that engages our passion and our talents? Whatever it is, we can count on the fact that it will give rise to problems and opposition. How we deal with that kind of trouble will be a test of our character and faith.

Coping with Resistance

This topic of how to cope with troubles and opposition is so important that we need to reflect further on it. In the case of Nehemiah, his challenges came both from without and within, just as today our workplace challenges come to us both from the outside — structures, the culture, and the "system," all part of the "principalities and powers" — as well as from within — boredom, criticism, faint-heartedness, discouragement.

The outside challenges for Nehemiah came from the surrounding peoples, most of them consumed with fear and envy of the rebuilding project. They attempted to humiliate the returned exiles. "What are those feeble Jews doing?" they asked, adding facetiously, "Even a fox climbing up would break down their wall of stones." Then they turned to threatening: "Before they know it or see us," they said, "we will be right there among them and will kill them and put an end to the work." How was Nehemiah going to deal with these threats? He dealt with them by praying and planning — two sides of leadership that is both godly and practical. He cried out to God and then reorganized the workers by having half of them guard the work and the other half do the actual building. When there was intrigue he refused to be distracted. "Come," the opponents said, "let us meet together in one of the villages." But Nehemiah refused to be drawn into the treachery. When there was false innuendo, as in the charge, "You are about to become king," he resolutely denied it. When there was intimidation, as in the invitation to seek refuge in the temple behind closed doors when the opponents sought to kill him, he said, "Should a man like me run away?"

But for all the external troubles, the inside challenges were even more difficult. Essentially the two problems Nehemiah faced among the people were the same as almost every leader faces today: discouragement and greed. Discouragement easily set in on account of physical exhaustion and the opponents' harassment. To deal with this situation, Nehemiah continued to hold up the vision to the people, to inspire faith, and to organize the workers for maximum security, some carrying a weapon with one hand

and working tools or materials with the other. But greed was an even harder challenge to cope with. Some of the well-to-do inhabitants took advantage of the situation by buying up fields and houses from their poorer neighbors, while other returning exiles had to sell their sons and daughters into slavery in order to survive. Nehemiah dealt with the situation by direct confrontation ("What you are doing is not right," he charged), by calling for restitution ("Give back to them immediately their fields," he demanded), and by his own generous example (feeding some of the people at the governor's table at his own expense).

So what do we learn from this inspiring story?

First, leadership is work and a work to which many are called — probably all of us, in fact. We all have a circle of influence, whether that circle is large or small.

Second, biblical leadership is more than serving people. It involves first of all being God's servant and therefore being at God's disposal to meet the needs of others, no matter how much it costs.

Third, we are created and called to take strategic initiative in whatever situation we find ourselves. This is what it means to be "shrewd" in biblical terms. It is the nature of the Father, Son, and Spirit to inspire creativity and risk-taking. Thus God's will is an empowering vision of greatness, inspiring initiative, creativity, and inventiveness.[2]

Fourth, we are providentially placed by God in situations where we can make a difference, whether these differences are small or great. God enlists each of us in a compelling project from which we must not be diverted. "I am carrying on a great project," was Nehemiah's perspective. The biblical way of describing this is commitment to building the realm of God. It embraces God's life-giving and transforming will in all of life. It links our jobs to the mighty purpose of God. The vision of sharing in God's great renewal project should capture us body and soul, a vision and project from which we must not be diverted, from which we "cannot

---

2. The crucial text on this in addition to Bernstein is Brian Griffiths, *The Creation of Wealth: A Christian's Case for Capitalism* (Downers Grove, Ill.: InterVarsity Press, 1984), chapter 3, "The Theological Dimension," pp. 40-63.

come down" (KJV), no matter what the troubles we face inside and out. And to do this, as we learn from Nehemiah, we must wisely and discreetly combine prayer — which nourishes our service to God and God's purposes — and planning — which is our practical way of serving people. And thus we can be as shrewd as snakes and as innocent as doves.

For Discussion and Reflection

Do you have a compelling project that has captured your heart, talents, time, and energy, one from which you "cannot come down"? If so, what are you doing about it? If not, how can you pray for such a project or passion to be given you?

9

Providential Work — Esther

The blue-collar blues is no more bitterly sung than the white-collar moan. "I'm a machine," says the spot-welder. "I'm caged," says the bank teller, and echoes the hotel clerk. "I'm a mule," says the steel worker. "A monkey can do what I do," says the receptionist. "I'm less than a farm implement," says the migrant worker. "I'm an object," says the high fashion model.

Studs Terkel, *Working*

At some time or other every one of us feels that we are in the wrong place, at the wrong time, doing the wrong thing. Maybe even married to the wrong person! We're tempted to think that if we were only somewhere else or doing something else, we could be useful and deeply satisfied. But the reality is that God has a providential purpose for our lives right where we are. And the Creator has been involved behind the scenes, as it were, in all the details of our everyday experiences as well as in our life-long work trajectory. The early desert fathers and mothers, those spiritual athletes who took to the desert to find God, often told one another, "Stay in your cell. It will teach you everything." Translated into contemporary English this means: "Don't go aimlessly from job to job looking for the perfect fit. There is a life-giving divine purpose in your life right where you are."

The Biblical Rags to Riches Story

No biblical story shows the need for single-minded commitment better than the story of a destitute Jewish girl who was thrust into the maws of a gigantic corporation. Esther, an orphan, raised by her cousin Mordecai during the Jewish exile in ancient Persia, was chosen for beauty treatments in preparation for her night with the king (who was looking for a new queen). Immediately her situation raises the question: Can God work through a pagan empire? A secular business? A beauty contest? A multinational corporation?

Each woman in the king's harem had a one-night stand with the monarch. After twelve months of preparation, Esther was ready for her debut with the king. It turned out that King Xerxes was "attracted to her more than any of the other women" and therefore chose her as his queen. But Esther, a Jew, and now queen in a pagan nation, kept her identity as a worshiper of the living God a secret. She did this at the direction of her cousin and adoptive father, Mordecai.

Mordecai kept in touch with his adopted daughter by spending time in the courtyard of the palace, where he uncovered a plot against the king himself. Through an intermediary he informed Esther of this, thus sparing the king's life. The king made a note of the incident in his journal but did nothing about it *at that moment.* Meanwhile, an egotistical Haman was promoted by the king to second in command, and he wanted everyone to bow down to him. Showing obeisance toward another human being, especially one as vile and self-centered as Haman, was something that Mordecai refused to do. Mordecai's behavior galled Haman deeply, and knowing that Mordecai was a Jew, Haman persuaded the king with a truth, a half-truth, and a lie (Esther 3:8-9) that the whole Jewish people scattered throughout the empire should be eliminated. Haman set a day for this holocaust and promised to pay for all the costs, no doubt a very attractive feature of his proposal to the king.

Mordecai heard of the edict, put on sackcloth, mourned, wept, and wailed. Eventually he got word to Esther, who apparently was unaware of the edict. His message to Esther was that she should go into the king's presence and beg for mercy for her people. She replied that she was not allowed to go into the king's presence, on pain of death, unless he lifted his golden scepter. Besides, it was now thirty days since the king had called for her. Mordecai's response to Esther is the centerpiece of the book:

> Do not think that because you are in the king's house you alone of all the Jews will escape. For if you remain silent at this time, relief and deliverance for the Jews will arise from another place, but you and your father's family will perish. And who knows but that you have come to royal position for such a time as this? (4:14)

For Such a Time as This

Mordecai's challenge prompted Esther to become an initiator. She took the risk of going to the king uncalled for. He raised his scepter and asked to know her request, offering her up to half of the realm. Cleverly, Esther invited the king to a feast at which she also included Haman, whom she knew to be the instigator of the plot against the Jews. So confident was she of her plan that at the time she spoke with the king she already had the feast prepared! At the feast King Xerxes asked her again to make her request known. This time she promised that at another feast the next day she would make her request fully known.

During the night, providentially, the king could not sleep and asked for some of the government records to be read to him. When he was reminded that Mordecai had saved his life he asked what had been done for him. "Nothing," was the answer. During the same night, ironically, Haman was boasting to his family and friends about how honored he had been to be the only person invited to Esther's banquet with the king and yet how incensed he was that Mordecai would not bow down to him. So he arranged to have a set of gallows built to hang Mordecai and planned to get the king's approval the next morning. He went early to the court and just as he entered the king asked, "What should be done for a person the king delights to honor?" Haman was so taken up with himself that he thought the king's question must relate to him in some way. So he said, "Have him ride on the king's horse and have someone go through the streets ahead and say, 'This is the person the king honors.'" "Well, you do it," said the king, "for Mordecai"!

Haman was humiliated and his friends told him that night, in so many words, that he was finished. Nonetheless, Haman rushed off to the second feast where Esther told the whole story and pleaded with the king, "Grant me my life. . . . Spare my people. . . . For I and my people have been sold to be destroyed, killed, and annihilated." In the process, Esther revealed her true identity as a worshiper of Yahweh. "Who is he? Where is he — the man who has dared to do such a thing?" asked the king. Esther answered, "An adversary and enemy! This vile Haman!" (7:3-6). Enraged, the king left the room to figure out what he would do because the laws of the Medes and Persians could not be changed. Meanwhile Haman fell on Queen Esther, reclining on her couch, and begged for mercy. Coming back in and finding Haman molesting his queen — or so it seemed — the king ordered him to be hanged on his own gallows, the gallows Haman had prepared for Mordecai. The multiple ironies in this story are a literary delight!

Mordecai then took Haman's place as second in command, just as Joseph, a Jew and worshiper of Yahweh, was placed in the second most powerful position in Egypt. For her part, Esther persuaded the king to arrange for a second edict, written this time by Mordecai, to allow the Jews to defend themselves on the day appointed for their destruction, a day selected by throwing dice (the *pur*, hence the celebration of the Jewish feast called Purim). The first edict could not be revoked but the second allowed the Jews to arm themselves to prevent the success of the first edict. Which is, in fact, what happened.

How Can Our Work Be Viewed as Providential?

First, providence means that God is involved in our work and workplace for his own good purpose. We can see divine providence in apparently haphazard events and choices made by human beings. But providence does not mean that human beings are helpless pawns being manipulated by a sovereign God. Human beings are, to a limited extent, free agents, responsible and accountable for their actions. So providence should be distinguished from erroneous teachings such as deism, which detaches God from the out-working of human destiny; fatalism, which depersonalizes human action into impersonal forces; and the popular notion of mere chance or luck. By contrast, divine providence asserts the directional and purposeful character of human history and personal destiny. It means that God is even more interested in our life-purpose than we are. As in the case of Esther and Mordecai, our lives are not a bundle of accidents. On the contrary, divine providence is at work in even seemingly meaningless or mundane moments.

Such an understanding of God's providential ordering of our lives should stimulate our confidence, gratitude, and faith. It means that God intends to bring the whole human story to a worthy end. This is reason enough to inspire hope and risk-taking. It means that even our mistakes get incorporated into God's overall purpose. Our career decisions are rarely irrevocable. To recognize this is to reduce the weight of decision-making. We are saved from arrogant egoism and cringing fear. A saying attributed to Søren Kierkegaard, the Danish philosopher, strikes a deep resonance with our experience: life is lived forward but understood backwards. Looking backwards on our lives, we can see the hand of God.

Second, providence means that where we are is not accidental. Providence means that our birthplace, family background, educational opportunities, the talents and abilities we bring to the workplace, even our physical or emotional disabilities, are not accidental but part of God's good and gracious purpose for us. Esther was strategically placed to be an influence. The Greek version of this book includes her prayers in which she tells the Lord how much she loathes the symbols of her position and the bed of the uncircumcised. We too are sent out Monday morning into schools, universities, hospitals, and businesses that may not share our faith in God. God has placed us in these significant locations "for such a time as this." Probably we will not understand it all at the time, just as Joseph did not discern until much later the providential purpose of his being rejected by his brothers, sold into slavery in Egypt, and then raised to senior governmental responsibility. "It was not you who sent me here, but God," Joseph said to his brothers (Gen. 45:8). Oswald Chambers says, "Never allow the thought — 'I am of no use where I am'; because you certainly cannot be of no use where you are not."[1] Francis de Sales wrote a classic guide to the ordinary person's spiritual life. In this book he says, "Great opportunities to serve God rarely present themselves, but little ones are frequent."[2]

That being said, there will come special times, times fraught with uncommon opportunity, which we must discern and resolve to seize. And it is in doing so that we will fulfill our mission. In this way we become priests of time, discerning the difference between clock time (which goes on and on, time that can be managed), and *kairos* time (time fraught with enormous consequences). Such opportunities arise in families, in businesses, in educational institutions, and in whole nations. Winston Churchill recognized the truth of this for his own life. He regarded his emergence into leadership in Britain during the Second World War as not only his, but also his nation's, finest hour. Our sovereign God is at work breaking into time and inviting us to seize the moment, celebrate the possibility, and respond to his gracious intervention. God is saying that there is something beautiful going on, as the Preacher in Ecclesiastes notes (3:11), something that calls forth an "Aha" moment.

But this hint about the beautiful moment points also, rather sadly, to its opposite: the possibility of not being present, of letting the present slip by without seeing its beauty, of being so future-oriented, so much on to the next thing, whether in business or in

---

1. Oswald Chambers, *My Utmost for His Highest* (Toronto: McClelland & Stewart, Ltd., 1953), p. 291.

2. Francis de Sales, *Introduction to the Devout Life*, trans. and ed. John K. Ryan (New York: Image Books, 2003), p. 202.

personal planning, that you are not really present at all — something I have personally had to wrestle with from time to time. At such times the notes of the eighteenth-century spiritual director Jean-Pierre de Caussade, originally published in English as *Self-Abandonment to Divine Providence,* have been a help to me. At one point he expresses this beautiful sentiment: "The sacrament of the present moment requires us to do our duty whatever it may be, a carrying out of God's purpose for us, not only this day, or this hour, but this minute, this very minute — now."[3]

The eighteenth-century poet William Cowper expressed similar thoughts. Cowper was subject to severe depression. One night in such a mood, when London was blanketed by fog, he called a cab and directed the escort to the Thames River where he planned to throw himself in. But try as he might, the driver could not find the river. Cowper grew more and more impatient until at last he leaped from the cab, determined to find his watery grave unassisted. Groping through the fog, to his utter amazement he found himself back on his own doorstep! Going to his room he penned the words of one of the famous Olney Hymns, "God Moves in a Mysterious Way." As one commentator has noted, Cowper wrote most of his hymns in the "red light of hell."[4]

> God moves in a mysterious way,
> His wonders to perform. . . .
>
> Judge not the Lord by feeble sense,
> But trust him for his grace;
> Behind a frowning providence
> He hides a smiling face.
>
> His purposes will ripen fast,
> Unfolding every hour;

3. Jean-Pierre de Caussade, *The Sacrament of the Present Moment,* trans. Kitty Muggeridge (Glasgow: Collins, 1981), p. 14.

4. Alexander M. Witherspoon, ed., *The College Survey of English Literature* (New York: Harcourt, Brace and Company, 1951), p. 635.

The bud may have a bitter taste,
But sweet will be the flower.

Blind unbelief is sure to err
And scan his work in vain;
God is his own interpreter,
And he will make it plain.[5]

For Discussion and Reflection

Referring to the saying of the Danish philosopher Søren Kierkegaard that life is lived forward but understood backward, trace the
hand of God's providence in your own life up to this point.

5. William Cowper, "Light Shining Out of Darkness," in Louis Bredvold et
al., eds., *Eighteenth Century Poetry and Prose,* 2nd ed. (New York: The Ronald
Press, 1956), pp. 884-85.

The Historical Books: A Brief Summary

What are some of the things we learn from the historical books? First, leadership is work. Hard but good work.

Second, leadership is critical in order for a group of people to grow to maturity and to thrive.

Third, leaders are stewards,[1] not masters of the people or their resources. They are called to exercise care and responsibility as they develop their people's potential for mission and productive work. Essentially, therefore, leaders are servants of the people.

Fourth, integrity and maturity are critical for leadership work since leaders not only exercise influence but also have a symbolic role. The primary factor that makes someone suited for leadership is his or her character.

Fifth, whether of small or large influence, leaders are providentially placed by God to make a difference.

---

1. See R. Paul Stevens, "Stewardship," in Robert Banks and R. Paul Stevens, eds., *The Complete Book of Everyday Christianity* (Downers Grove, Ill.: InterVarsity Press, 1997), pp. 962-67, and Peter Block, *Stewardship: Choosing Service over Self-Interest* (San Francisco: Berrett-Koehler, 1993).

PART THREE

Soul Work

An Introduction to the Wisdom Books

I discovered and am still discovering up to this very moment that it is only by living completely in this world that one learns to believe. . . . It is in such a life that we throw ourselves utterly into the arms of God.

Dietrich Bonhoeffer, *Letters and Papers from Prison*

If in the previous sections we have seen many concrete and colorful examples of people living out their faith as both saints and workers, in this next section we will encounter many examples of people reflecting deeply on the issues of life and calling. In the Psalms we are privileged to overhear the prayers of persons, sometimes even of a whole people. In the book of Proverbs we see the writer crafting images and wise sayings on which we are intended to ruminate. In this way revelation sneaks through our self-justifying and prideful defenses. As for its relevance to work, this part of the Bible often speaks to us indirectly yet clearly about what work means for real people. These teachings come to us through the stories of people like the sufferer Job, and the professor in the book of Ecclesiastes, and, not least, through King Solomon, who in the Proverbs reflects on the character of both the sluggard and the entrepreneurial businessperson. J. I. Packer paraphrases a famous devotional writer's comments on this section of the Bible: "The Psalter teaches you how to pray and praise, Prov-

81

erbs teaches you how to behave, Job teaches you how to suffer, the Song of Solomon teaches you how to love, and Ecclesiastes teaches you how to enjoy."[1]

Biblical Wisdom

A word needs to be said about the term *wisdom* itself. The Hebrew word *hokmah* has a far wider range of meanings than is normally associated with the English word "wisdom." The Old Testament concept of *wisdom* encompasses a realistic approach to many of the problems of life, being applied as it is to artists, craftspeople (Exod. 28:3), musicians, singers, weavers (Exod. 35:25), and sailors (Ezek. 27:8), as well as those skilled in the conduct of war and in the administration of the state (1 Kings 3:12). In chapter 5 I wrote about Bezalel and his associates, who were described in the book of Exodus as being "filled with wisdom" (Exod. 35:31). In short, wisdom is practical know-how about life and work.[2] Biblical wisdom is roughly equivalent to biblical theology. It is not merely information but, as the Puritan William Perkins said of theology itself, it is "the science of living blessedly forever."[3] Wisdom is a way of life that is God-originated, God-oriented, and God-pleasing.

The Psalms

The Psalms do not offer direct teaching on work, but from time to time they reflect on human beings engaged in work, especially David. Essentially, the Psalms are the combined prayer and hymn book of Israel. But there is an extraordinary message in the

1. J. I. Packer, "Theology and Wisdom," in J. I. Packer and Sven Soderlund, eds., *The Way of Wisdom: Essays in Honor of Bruce K. Waltke* (Grand Rapids: Zondervan, 2000), pp. 1-14.

2. Robert Gordis, *Koheleth: The Man and His World* (New York: Shocken Books, 1951/68), pp. 16-17.

3. William Perkins, *A Golden Chain,* cited in Ian Breward, ed., *The Work of William Perkins* (Abingdon, U.K.: Sutton Courtenay Press, 1970), p. 17.

Psalms that bears on the theology and spirituality of work. Authored largely but not totally by David, the Psalms contain the most honest and startling confessions ("Against you only have I sinned"), complaints ("God, wake up!"), longings ("As the deer pants for the water brook, so I long for you, God"), petitions (essentially saying, "Things are really going wrong, God; what can you do about it?"), and thanksgivings ("You have delivered my soul from death and my eyes from tears"). In these honest and heartfelt utterances, the psalmist is essentially saying that *we have the kind of God to whom we can say anything.* God positively invites this kind of honesty, awakens it, inspires it, and responds to it. We can tell the whole truth of our lives to God. And this "whole truth" can include how we feel about work and how we experience our work.

Most of the psalms attributed to David reveal him fighting an enemy, seen or unseen. "Lord, how many are my foes!" (Ps. 3:1), he cries. And that is one of the realities of the work world: it inevitably entails opposition from the principalities and powers (Eph. 6:12, KJV), evil spirits, human enemies, and corrupted structures. Therefore, as we saw in Genesis chapters 3 and 4, any theology of work must take into account the fact that work in this world — at least until Christ comes again — is hard. But that is only one side of the story. There are other books besides the Psalms in the wisdom section.

A Strange Book about Play

While we will soon turn to a closer analysis of the stories of Job, the professor in Ecclesiastes, and the sluggard and the entrepreneurial woman in Proverbs, in the meantime we should also say something about the enigmatic book of Song of Solomon or, as it is sometimes called, the Song of Songs. Like other books in this section, this one, too, in a strange way says something about work. Work as we have defined it is energy expended *purposefully,* whether manual, mental, or both. By contrast, play is simply enjoyed for its own sake. It is not utilitarian. To be authentic, a biblical theology of work must also explore the counterpoise of work, namely leisure, play, rest, and Sabbath. The line between them is not always clear, but the fact that we need both is clearly indicated in the divinely directed word on work in both Genesis and the Ten Commandments.

The Song of Songs is an unusual book about love-play and erotic love. Understandably, celibate monks like Saint Bernard who spent their lives expounding this book sought to avoid its plain meaning by treating it as an allegory of Christ's love for the church. An elderly saint, whose name I have now forgotten, once said to me, "Only someone with a dirty mind could read this book as anything other than an allegory of Christ's love for the church." The truth of the matter, however, is that in its original setting, this book is about the beauty of playful, erotic love. Admittedly, it is not really a book about work, though one could argue that Solomon made a consuming profession out of acquiring new wives and enjoying them sexually — hundreds of them, in fact! Although he did indulge this "profession" with a vengeance, the particular story narrated in this "Song" is not simply about Solomon adding yet another young woman to his harem. Rather, it is the story of a triangle of lovers: Solomon, a lovely but dark country girl called the "Shulammite," and a second man, a country shepherd to whom the woman is betrothed and whom, in fantasy or fact, she seeks, finds, and loves.

In the book, Solomon objectifies the woman, describing her anatomically. But the woman longs for her true lover who embraces her as a person, not just a body. In the end, whether in a dream or reality, the country shepherd in effect says that while Solomon may have his many wives, for his part he is content with only one. She is enough. This attitude is in high contrast to the display of Solomon's lust throughout the book, something which initially catches us by surprise. But it is there. On the other hand, wholesome marital love is something quite different. As Calvin Seerveld says, "Scripture affirms and unashamedly encourages bodily celebration of human love, but severely rejects Solomon's practice of lust. When passion becomes fixed in a grasping adoration and [Yahweh's] created ordinances for the caresses of love are broken, then the passion is evil."[4] So while the Song of Songs may well have a secondary meaning as an example of God's love for his people, its first meaning is to exalt the beauty and purity of erotic love and love-play between committed covenant partners.

Now what does all this have to do with a theology of work? For one thing, our work inevitably has a sexual dimension, especially when we work with people of the other sex, some of whom we find attractive. We have to admit that the workplace can be erotic. But in a strange way, even work itself can become erotic. For some people, workaholism provides an alternative ecstasy. In an insightful section in her book on workaholism, a section entitled "Erotica," Barbara Killinger compares work experiences with sexual orgasms: "When there is a passionate obsession with work, erotic feelings can be expressed towards the accomplishments or products of work. . . . Failing to find the divine source of legitimate ecstasy, people find unsatisfactory substitutes."[5] The irony in all of this, of course, is that while some people become workaholics, others take play and rest to the extreme and become play-a-holics, especially in the retirement years.

There is yet one more dimension to recognize in a biblical theology of work: Just as love in a covenant relationship is embodied emotionally and physically, so work for God's realm is not merely spiritual but also holistic, human, and embodied.[6] Unfortunately, for centuries the church has been infected with Neo-Platonic dualism, which teaches that the spirit is holy but the body is profane, a teaching that is, paradoxically, a serious hindrance to spiritual growth and maturity. The consequences of this body-rejecting dualism for a proper understanding of the dignity and meaning of work have been disastrous. I therefore urge you to read all the wisdom books and let their invigorating stories inform your heart and mind and, not least, your work life.

4. Calvin Seerveld, *The Greatest Song: In Critique of Solomon* (Palos Heights, Ill.: Trinity Pennyasheet Press, 1963/7), p. 72.

5. Barbara Killinger, *Workaholics: The Respectable Addicts* (New York: Simon and Schuster, 1991), p. 34.

6. See Hans Walter Wolff, *Anthropology of the Old Testament*, trans. Margaret Kohl (Philadelphia: Fortress Press, 1974).

10

Wild Work — God and Job

If the rain falls on bleak moors, this is not because of any necessity but because it pleases God. Utility is not the primary reason for God's action; the creative breath of God is inspired by beauty and joy. Job is invited to sing with Yahweh the wonders of creation — without forgetting that the source of it all is the free and gratuitous love of God.

Gustavo Gutiérrez, *Job: God-Talk
and the Suffering of the Innocent*

Towards the end of the fascinating though ancient book of Job — so ancient that neither the temple in Jerusalem nor the law given to Moses is mentioned in it — Job makes this remarkable statement, "My ears had heard of you but now my eyes have seen you. Therefore I despise myself and repent in dust and ashes" (Job 42:5-6). But this declaration raises the intriguing question, "Of what was it that Job repented?" The question is especially pertinent since Job's offer to repent comes after he has been confronted with God's wild creation and God's wild work.

The Duel

The story starts with God and Satan discussing the character of this truly extraordinary person. God thinks he has a winner — a man who is "blameless and upright," someone "who fears God and shuns evil" (1:8). Satan, however, the master of accusation, taunts God with the suggestion that Job has ulterior motives for being so upright and respectful of God. "Does Job fear God for nothing?" Satan asks in his conniving way (1:9). The issue is whether Job's faith is genuine or gratuitous; that is, whether he is upright and holy because of his integrity of character or because of what he gets out of the relationship with God, the reward of a commercial contract negotiated with the deity. Satan's subtle reasoning goes like this: Job gives God reverence and God gives Job a beautiful family, meaningful work, respect in the community, health, and wealth. It is this provocative challenge to Job's integrity of character that gives rise to a great duel between Satan and God in which God allows Satan to take away everything Job has, except his life. But it is also at this point where Job's friends come in.

They mean well. Job is suffering excruciating pain. They come to visit Job, sitting silently in the ash heap with him. But when they finally speak they try to explain Job's suffering using the orthodoxy of the day. Job, they say, is suffering because either he or members of his family are sinners. Evidently Job's friends are threatened by what they cannot fully understand or by the fear that the same thing could happen to them. As a result, they start to attack Job rather than to comfort him, though ironically, by forcing Job to engage them in debate they may well be keeping him from committing suicide! Their strategy is to try to convince Job of his sin and guilt, but instead of producing guilt in the sufferer as intended, the "God-talking" friends provoke Job to vigorous self-justification.

Here is where the story becomes remarkable and revelatory. Against the attack of his so-called "comforters," Job takes his appeal to the highest court of all — to God. He insists, in a "gospel-in-advance" kind of intuition, that if God were human he could surely find a solution for his suffering (9:32-35). Perhaps, Job thinks, he has a kinsman-redeemer — a close relative in heaven — who could plead his case (16:15-21) and ultimately enable him to see God, even after his own skin had been destroyed (19:23-27). Providentially, it seems, he thus stumbled on the gospel of Jesus centuries before Jesus was born.

Job, the True Theologian

At the end of the narrative God speaks to Job's friends. Although their speeches might have been published in an orthodox Christian journal, yet God says to them, "You have not spoken of me what is right, as my servant Job has" (42:7). What, then, was wrong? Just this: the friends spoke *about* God to Job in ways that were totally predictable and culturally conditioned. Job spoke *to* God, even in his blustering, heaven-pounding prayers. And the true theologian — one who "speaks well of God" — is one who prays. The theologian P. T. Forsyth says, "Does not Christ set more value upon importunity than on submission?" Forsyth refers to the parable of the unjust judge, the plea of the Syrophoenician woman, Paul's threefold petition to be released from his "thorn," Moses interceding for Israel, Jacob wrestling with the angel, and Abraham pleading, yes haggling, with God for Sodom. In the case of Job, Forsyth describes him as brazenly "facing God, withstanding Him, almost bearding Him and extracting revelation."[1] The conclusion of the matter is that prayer, not God-talk, is what Job or any other suffering person needs.

After Job's agonizing attempts at self-justification and his importunate pleading with God, the Ruler of creation finally is revealed to Job in a whirlwind. In relentless cross-examination, God asks Job whether he can match God's wild work in creation. "Who is this that obscures my plans with words without knowledge?" God asks. "Where were you when I laid the earth's foundation?" (38:2-4). Who invented patterns of time? "Have you ever given orders to the morning" (38:12)? Who is the master of the weather? "Have you entered the storehouses of the snow or seen the store-

---

1. P. T. Forsyth, *The Soul of Prayer* (London: Independent Press, 1954), p. 86.

houses of the hail?" (38:22). Who sustains the universe? "Can you bring forth the constellations in their seasons?" (38:32). Who maintains life systems on earth? "Do you know when the mountain goats give birth?" (39:1). Is everything designed to serve human beings? "Will the wild ox consent to serve you?" (39:9). "Do you have an arm like God's and can your voice thunder like his?" (40:9). So we come back to the question, What was it that Job repented of?

Job repented of believing in a small God. He repented of attempting to control God even in his theology (in fact, just as his friends had tried to do). And what happened in Job's heart was not the cringing repentance his friends sought but something much more redemptive and more universally relevant. Job turned from not letting God be God, of not loving God for God's sake. Thus, in extracting revelation from God, in his passionate search for friendship with God, in his unwillingness to let God go unless God blessed him, Job was brought in his dark blustering prayers, without his even knowing it, to the feet of Jesus, the God-man, the Kinsman-Redeemer in heaven whom he would see with his own eyes (42:5).

God's Wild Work

All this teaches us that God was working even before there were human beings. God works when humans cannot work. God does work that human beings cannot do. And God's work is wild. It is untamable. Utterly uncontrollable. Majestic. Awesome. No wonder David Strong waxes eloquent about God's creative activity when he writes:

> Wild things in this passage do not need to be rearranged, "developed," or made use of before they reach the fullness of their being. Wild things in these passages are already as good as they can be, on their own. Recognizing them in their own right, pausing and lingering unselfconsciously before them, makes one receptive to a fresh and refreshing vision of our existence.[2]

2. David Strong, "The Promise of Technology versus God's Promise in Job," *Theology Today* 48, no. 2 (July 1991): 174.

In contrast, human technology promises to bring everything under our control, to make life good through the provision of goods, and so to bring happiness. Unlike human technology, the vision of God's wild work in Job 38–41 shows us the limits of human creativity and ought to bring a new respect for God's wild creation. In responding with worship and wonder we will discover, as Job did, that God's work is beautiful, that God's very self is beautiful. In a remarkable commentary on Job, liberation theologian Gustavo Gutiérrez says that the deepest answer to Job's questions and his prayers is not a rational explanation of the justice of God or a plausible explanation of the problem of pain. The deepest answer to the mystery of suffering lies in contemplation of God himself, attending to the qualities of God's goodness and greatness.[3]

In his pastoral commentary on Job, William Hulme notes, "After his encounter [with God] Job still does not know the *why*. Yet he seems to accept the *how*. The reason — he knows the *Who*. He who knows the *Who*, therefore can bear with any *how* even though he knows not the *why*. Knowing the *Who* without knowing the *why* leaves room for faith. It brings security without having answers."[4]

What, then, does all this mean for human work?

First, it means that human work is a pale imitation of God's own work, never as wild, never as awesome, never as worthy of contemplation. Job is healed not by being humiliated but by meditating on the character of God. He is healed by the beauty of God. He is healed in the contemplation of God's wilderness. According to Strong, what finally heals Job is the "fresh vision of things in their created wildness, in their being what they are, quite apart from both being for us or being assisted by us."[5]

Second, human work is limited. We do not have absolute control

---

3. Gustavo Gutiérrez, *Job: God-Talk and the Suffering of the Innocent* (Maryknoll, N.Y.: Orbis Books, 1988), p. 87.

4. William E. Hulme, *Dialog in Despair: Pastoral Commentary on the Book of Job* (New York: Abingdon Press, 1963), p. 146.

5. Strong, "The Promise of Technology," p. 179.

over creation. The promise of technology is complex. Job himself reflects on the technology of mining in chapter 28 but only to show how much more difficult it is to gain wisdom. Technology is one of the principalities and powers and it, like all the powers, is not neutral. It claims a certain allegiance that properly belongs to God and must be both exposed and redeemed. We use technology in a redemptive way when we show utter respect for the creation of God and do not try to make or control something.

Third, in our daily work, we do well to remember that everything is not for us, for our *development, improvement, or self-indulgence.* Everything does not need to be useful. Or as Gustavo Gutiérrez says, "Utility is not the primary reason for God's action."[6] Nor is it necessarily the primary reason for human work. Sometimes God waters "a land where no one lives" (38:26). Everything is not for our use. This realization should lead to humility in work and freedom from the tyranny of utility. Everything in creation is for God and God's pleasure.

So, how do we get a biblical view of work? Take a tour of some undeveloped creation, go on a canoe trip, climb a mountain, or take an African safari and take the book of Job with you.[7]

For Discussion and Reflection

"God was working even before there were human beings. God works when humans cannot work. God does work that human beings cannot do" (p. 89). Unpack these three statements by giving concrete examples of the work that God does.

How does exploring God's wild work affect your perspective on human work?

---

6. Gutiérrez, *Job,* p. 75. On the question of inutility, see the brilliant essay by Jacques Ellul, *The Politics of God and the Politics of Man,* trans. Geoffrey W. Bromiley (Grand Rapids: Eerdmans, 1972), pp. 190-99.

7. R. Paul Stevens, "The Song of the Paddle," in Byron Rempel-Burkholder and Dora Dueck, eds., *Northern Lights: An Anthology of Contemporary Christian Writing in Canada* (Mississauga, Ont.: John Wiley and Sons, 2008), pp. 17-21.

11

Slothful Work — The Sluggard

There are few things I hate more than laziness. I work very, very hard and I expect the people who work for me to do the same. If you want to succeed, you cannot relax. . . . I never take vacations because I can't handle the time away from my work. I recently read that these days, a high percentage of the people who do take vacations tend to check email and voicemail and call in to the office when they leave. Those are the people I want working for me.

Donald Trump, The Trump Blog, October 10, 2007

Sluggard. It's such an ugly word, suggestive of that barely-moving, gooey slug that crawls along the ground with imperceptible motion. Unfortunately, some people are like that, sluggish, lazy, and indolent. No wonder Proverbs has so much to say about this theme.[1] Sluggards dip their hands in the bowl but are so lazy they can't bring their hands to their mouths (Prov. 19:24). They are married to their beds, groaning when they turn over like a squeaky door as it rotates in its socket (26:14). They won't get up because they pretend there is danger out there, maybe a lion in the

---

1. There are fourteen references to the Hebrew word (6:6, 9; 10:26; 13:4; 15:19; 19:24; 20:4; 21:25; 22:13; 24:30; 26:13, 14, 15, 16, plus a couple of related noun references in 19:15 and 31:27) with the basic meaning of "lazy."

streets (22:13). They don't plant seeds in the critical growing season, yet go out at harvest time to look, only to find nothing (20:4). In short, Proverbs provides both humorous and devastating word pictures of the sluggard, since the first thing that strikes us about these pictures is their absurdity, followed by the realization that these pictures actually amount to thorough condemnations of these idlers. These pictures tell us how not to work and explain why some people do not "get into" their work. Are we meant to laugh our way into the realm of God on seeing these ludicrous pictures — and repenting?

Those unfortunate enough to employ a sluggard will discover that such a person is "dead weight." In his commentary on the book of Proverbs, Derek Kidner notes succinctly that sluggards "will not begin things . . . will not finish things . . . will not face things. . . . Consequently [they are] *restless* (13:4; 21:25, 26) with unsatisfied desire; *helpless* in the face of the tangle of [their] affairs, which are like a 'hedge of thorns' (15:19); and *useless* — expensively (18:9) and exasperatingly (10:26) — to any who must employ [them]."[2] The sluggard knows nothing of the creation mandate, that work is good, that work is part of our God-imaging dignity, and that there is no concept of retirement in the Bible. In short, the idler has no theology of work. Realizing neither the intrinsic value nor the extrinsic value of work, the sluggard refuses to see work as a gift, a calling, and a blessing. Work is good in itself — it has intrinsic value. Also, work is good for what it leads to — harvests, provision, and helping others, which is a ministry — the extrinsic value. By contrast, the sluggard is imprisoned in his or her own self. That is why simple physical lethargy does not get to the root problem. The sluggard may have strong desire (13:4) but for the wrong things. The longings are deadly (21:25) and they lead to the futile pursuit of emptiness (12:11).

---

2. Derek Kidner, *Proverbs* (Downers Grove, Ill.: InterVarsity Press, 1963), pp. 42-43.

Degrees of Sloth

So what is the problem? Is it simply physical sluggishness? Or is it deeper — spiritual and theological? As we will see, it really is a heart problem, which manifests itself in various ways.

First there is *physical sloth,* that is, bodily inertia, not caring to get up and go, rotating in bed like a squeaky door hinge. The Puritans were particularly descriptive of this as one of the "deadlies." Richard Baxter distinguishes idleness and sloth in this way: "Sloth signifieth chiefly the indisposition of the mind and body; and idleness signifieth the actual neglect or omission of our duties. Sloth is an averseness to labor, through a carnal love of ease, or indulgence to the flesh. . . . Sloth is easily identified: when the very thought of labor is troublesome, when ease seems sweet, when the easy part of some duty is culled out, when you work with a constant weariness of mind, when you consistently offer excuses or delays and when little impediments stop you."[3] In short, physical sloth is not getting up and going.

Mental sloth is a failure of imagination. When we work, we create things twice, first in the "mind's eye" and then in the outer world. But sluggards don't "see" what work needs to be done, nor can they see the fatal outcome of not working. They are mentally blind. They are surprised to find no harvest, surprised that poverty comes on them as a thief.

Moral sloth is failing to care in the right direction, failing to address the ethical requirements of life, including providing for oneself and caring for one's neighbor. In contrast, the sages in Proverbs put the emphasis on ethical action that proceeds from a virtuous character. "The way of the sluggard is blocked with thorns," but by contrast "the path of the upright [that is, the virtuous person] is a highway" (15:19). Such a morally upright person is the one truly marked by wisdom.

Spiritual sloth, commonly called *acedia,* is not caring about God and God's purposes. It is heart failure. *Acedia* is sometimes

---

3. Richard Baxter, *The Practical Works of Richard Baxter,* vol. 1 (Ligonier, Pa.: Soli Deo Gloria Publications, 1990), part 1, x, p. 378.

called the "noonday demon" because it attacks monks in the heat of day and makes them hate their cells, their work, their spiritual disciplines, even reading the Bible and praying, and, worst of all, it makes them hate themselves.[4] St. Augustine called *acedia* "the sadness of goodness and the joy of evil." It is a kind of lingering suicide. Dorothy Sayers said that sloth "is the sin that believes nothing, cares about nothing, seeks to know nothing, loves nothing, hates nothing, finds purpose in nothing . . . and remains alive because there is nothing for which one will die."[5] In fact, spiritual sloth is the root of all the other manifestations of sloth and therefore points to the ultimate healing of the sluggard.

Healing Acedia

Dispersed throughout Proverbs' collection of aphorisms is the proposition that if you have wisdom — that is, practical know-how about life in the light of God's covenant relationship with people — you will not be a sluggard. Conversely, if you are a sluggard, what you need is wisdom. The sluggard needs a converted heart, the heart trained in priorities, passion, decisiveness, and prayer. How does one acquire such wisdom?

The early monks took to the desert because the church was respectable, wealthy, and top-heavy with clergy. What they discovered when they went to the Egyptian desert is that with the reduction of external distractions — wealth, pleasure, and power — they had to deal with the increase of internal distractions, with their thought-life. The fourth-century monk Evagrius came to see the importance of recognizing which thoughts were constructive and which ones were destructive. This led the monks to speak of confronting the demons, which in our terminology refers to "per-

---

4. Paul Jordan-Smith, "Seven (and more) Deadly Sins," *Parabola* 10 (Winter 1985): 45. See also R. Paul Stevens and Alvin Ung, *Taking Your Soul to Work* (Grand Rapids: Eerdmans, 2010), chapter 6.

5. Quoted in Kathleen Norris, *Acedia and Me: A Marriage, Monks, and a Writer's Life* (New York: Penguin Books, 2008), p. 306.

sonal issues," or destructive inner thoughts. This is what sluggards (and other life-avoiding people) need to do. They need to seek solitude and confront the false self so that the true self can be born. In the monastic tradition, that kind of rebirth has been called *continuing conversion.*

As with all true conversion, continuing conversion is both a gift and an accomplishment. It requires a symphony of wills — God's and ours — agreeing to bring about a new heart. Only when the sluggard really wants such a change is there hope for "conversion." To begin with it need be only a faint prayer amplified in God's wide and generous hearing heart. Then those who would be converted must take up the disciplines of responsiveness: waiting on God and confronting self in solitude, cultivating new thoughts about work (both its intrinsic and extrinsic value), taking decisive action even when they don't feel like it, and reminding themselves continuously for Whom it is they are working.

For Discussion and Reflection

As suggested by Donald Trump's quote at the beginning of this chapter, workaholism — that respectable addiction — is really the dark side of sloth — moral sloth. Once again the person is cocooned in one's self, meeting deep needs for significance by performance and having no care for the neighbor, which might even be spouse and family. To live for work or to live for nonwork are two sides of the same coin.[6] Kathleen Norris has named the connection between sloth and workaholism. "Acedia, as sloth's spiritual manifestation, is deceptively contradictory, and a compulsive productivity can be one of its masks."[7] Discuss her proposition.

---

6. See R. Paul Stevens, "Drivenness," in Robert Banks and R. Paul Stevens, eds., *The Complete Book of Everyday Christianity* (Downers Grove, Ill.: InterVarsity Press, 1997), pp. 312-18.

7. Norris, *Acedia and Me*, p. 160.

12

Entrepreneurial Work — The Businessperson

[There can be] no capitalist development without an entre-
preneurial class; no entrepreneurial class without a moral
charter; no moral charter without religious premises.

Gianfranco Poggi, *Calvinism and the Capitalist Spirit:*
Max Weber's Protestant Ethic

Some might call Proverbs 31:10-31 one of the "texts of terror" since
it seems to describe a superwoman in comparison with whom
other women may feel they fade into insignificance. After all, as
the text itself asks (31:10), "Who can find such a woman?" It is an
apt question. The answer is, "No one." Instead, this word picture
offers an idealized model, not a flesh and blood example. Certainly the passage should not be used to critique or measure a
woman's worth, especially that of one's wife. In the Old Testament, the picture drawn here is demonstrated in the life of Ruth, a
truly "noble" woman (Ruth 3:11), who embodied many of the
characteristics of the entrepreneurial woman of Proverbs 31, as
well as by the beautiful Shulammite in the Song of Songs, who was
the initiator of an affectionate covenant relationship.

But even if the entrepreneurial woman of Proverbs 31 is only
an idealized picture, we still want to ask what we can learn from
this impressive passage. And specifically we want to ask what con-
tribution this half-chapter makes to a theology of work — for

women *and* for men. Earlier we discovered that both biblical theology and biblical wisdom are, as Puritan theologian William Perkins defined them, "the science of living blessedly forever." If this is so, then here is a woman who surely embodies both living and working blessedly.

First, the ideal woman of Proverbs 31 is working for the benefit of others. This woman brings her husband "good, not harm" (31:12). She gets wool and flax to make clothes for her family (31:13). She works with her hands to make things she can sell in the market, "like the merchant ships, bringing her food from afar" (31:14), exchanging her hand-made products for household necessities (31:24). Not only have her children benefited from her industry, but her husband is enabled to do business and give leadership at the town gate, to be a community leader (31:23). Further, she is sensitive to the needs of the less fortunate: "She opens her arms to the poor and extends her hands to the needy" (31:20). Her children and husband rise up to call her blessed (31:28).

Second, she is entrepreneurial. Defining entrepreneurship is not an easy task. *Entrepreneur* is a French term that in the Middle Ages was used of a cleric who was in charge of a great architectural work such as a cathedral or a castle. In this one person were combined the functions of inventor, planner, architect, manager, employer, and supervisor. Essentially, therefore, entrepreneurship involves three facets — envisioning, inventing, and implementing — all of which are equally necessary for an activity to be fully entrepreneurial.

As an entrepreneur, then, this noble woman "considers a field and buys it; out of her earnings she plants a vineyard" (31:16). She develops it and makes it profitable. This instinct for shrewd business practice comes not out of existential anxiety, as nineteenth-century political economist Max Weber proposed in his famous thesis on capitalism, nor out of a fear of failure and rejection as exemplified by the one-talent-man in Jesus' parable of the talents (Matt. 25:24-25). Rather, the noble woman, and those who follow her, is not motivated by fear of divine rejection but by the opposite — by affectionate reverence for God.

Weber's thesis can be summarized in this way: For capitalism to flourish there must be both intense commercial activity and the imperative to save. Weber traced the rise of both motivations to Calvinism. As for commercial activity, Weber argued that instead of finding acceptance with God through the monasteries, true believers were now enjoined to prove themselves by intensive work in the world. As for the imperative to save, Weber saw that Calvinism taught self-denial and delayed gratification, both essential elements for the accumulation of capital. Furthermore, according to Weber, the theological underpinnings for this system were supplied by Calvin's twin doctrines of transcendence and predestination. God's transcendence and human predestination increase the tension and anxiety (that is, whether someone is indeed among the elect), while the doctrine of calling to this-worldly work and not just religious activity "opens the believer to the world."[1]

While elements of Weber's thesis ring true, the biblical entrepreneurial spirit comes from the triune God who inspires risk-taking, experimentation, and creative initiative. Both Luther and Calvin called people to the foundational document of the Christian faith — the Bible — and to the essential Gospel experience. Thus they argued that the primary spiritual posture — and therefore the psychological force for life in this world — was not existential anxiety (the fear of being rejected by God); rather, true spirituality consists of a combination of *gratitude* to God and *love* of neighbor. These are the sources of real entrepreneurship, inspiring people to creative action, to dream dreams, and to serve the common good.[2]

Third, the noble woman is hard-working. We read that "Her lamp does not go out at night" (31:18) and that she "does not eat the bread of idleness" (31:27). While this could mean that she is a workaholic or overly career-oriented, the truth is probably otherwise. In fact, evidence suggests that far from being career-oriented

1. Max Weber, *The Protestant Ethic and the Spirit of Capitalism*, trans. Talcott Parsons (New York: Charles Scribner's Sons, 1958), p. 70.

2. This connection between the triune God and co-creativity with God is explored in the classic book by Sir Brian Griffiths, *The Creation of Wealth*, and a more recent book by Peter Bernstein, *Against the Gods: The Remarkable Story of Risk*, both noted in previous chapters.

she is actually *other-oriented* and her industriousness is not a response to some unmet need for acceptance or approval but is motivated by her neighborliness, her obedience to the second great commandment — that of loving the neighbor. And this love of neighbor, as we shall see, is in turn motivated by the first commandment, wholehearted love of God.

Fourth, she has joy in her work. The statement in 31:13 that she "works with eager hands" can also be translated, "She works with her hands *with pleasure*."[3] There are multiple joys in work: the joy of simply being able to work, the joy of using gifts and talents, and the joy of simply knowing that others will benefit from our work. But the ultimate joy in work, here hinted at in the reference to our ideal woman being "a woman who fears the LORD" (31:30), is to work gladly in God's name and for God's sake. Her motivation comes from a relationship of affectionate reverence of God, being taught by God in life, illustrated by the servant in Isaiah who says, "The Sovereign LORD has given me a well-instructed tongue. . . . He wakens me morning by morning, wakens my ear to listen like one being instructed" (Isa. 50:4).[4] This is essentially the spirituality of work that Jesus teaches at the close of one of his parables when he says, "Come and share your master's happiness" (Matt. 25:23). As a sign of this pleasure, the woman of Proverbs makes fine clothing for herself — Egyptian linen and purple (Prov. 31:22), materials suggestive of royalty. She also makes beautiful bed coverings for "her bed" (31:22), a delicate phrase that may well have sensual overtones.[5]

Fifth, the work of this noble woman reflects an interior beauty of character. The writer of Proverbs says that "She is clothed with strength and dignity" (31:25) and that "Her husband has full confidence in her" (31:11). Once again we see that the heart is the core personality. The husband has entrusted his heart to her, knowing

---

3. Tremper Longman III, *Proverbs* (Grand Rapids: Baker, 2006), p. 543.

4. Bruce Waltke, "The Fear of the Lord: The Foundation for a Relationship with God" in J. I. Packer and Loren Wilkinson, eds. *Alive to God: Studies in Spirituality* (Downers Grove, Ill.: InterVarsity Press, 1992), pp. 17-33.

5. Longman, *Proverbs*, p. 545.

that he will not be abused, manipulated, or disappointed. Her interior perfectly matches her exterior in a winsome integrity. "She speaks with wisdom, and faithful instruction is on her tongue" (31:26). Here is a woman who is not timid, not sheepishly compliant to her husband, not frivolous, but truly beautiful in every area of her life.

In conclusion, the noble woman exemplifies the creation mandate of which we took note in Genesis 1. She unfolds the potential of creation and is a steward of the resources with which God has trusted her. She also builds community through her work, both within her family and more widely through provision and care for the poor. And finally her work is inundated with reverence for God, the third part of the creation mandate. Just as Adam and Eve prior to the fall undertook the rule of creation in the fear of God, so the wise woman lives and works in the fear of God.

An impossible model to copy in every detail? Yes. An inspiring ideal to reach for? Most certainly.

For Discussion and Reflection

How do you react to this picture of the noble woman? What characteristics of her style of work are transferable to your own work situation, whether you are male or female?

People "work hard" for many reasons. It is often described as the "work ethic" of a particular culture. For what good reasons should we work hard? When do we work too hard? And why?

13

Enigmatic Work — The Professor

In spite of God's respect and love for man, in spite of God's extreme humility in entering into man's projects, in the long run one cannot but be seized by a profound sense of the inutility and vanity of human action.

Jacques Ellul, "Meditation on Inutility"

"Do you like your new job?" It was a foolish question, a very Western question to ask a Kenyan. But Esther had been my student in a rural theological college in East Africa for three years. Like the others, she had hoped, upon graduation, to be placed as a pastor of a church. Instead she was given the enormously demanding task of being matron for three hundred girls in a boarding school. It was a twenty-four-hours-a-day, seven-days-a-week job with little recognition and limited remuneration. So I had reason to ask. But her answer revealed a deep spirituality and a work ethic that I covet for Christians in my home country and for myself. She said, "*I like it in Jesus.*" She might have said, "I am enduring it for Jesus' sake," or "It is not what I would have chosen but I am trying to accept it." But to "like it in Jesus" is the soul of work and anticipates lessons to be discovered in this chapter, even if they are embedded in an enigmatic source like the Old Testament book of Ecclesiastes.

The Dilemma of Work

One notable fact about Scripture is the way it often poses penetrating questions to the reader. One such question asked by the Professor in the Old Testament book of Ecclesiastes is very probing indeed and relates directly to our theme: "What do people get for all the toil and anxious striving with which they labor under the sun?" (Eccles. 2:22). The inspired author, probably someone of considerable means who has taken on the persona of King Solomon, is genuinely searching for an answer. This question plumbs the depths of our experience of work. It is a question asked not only by people at the end of a long hard day at the office or home, or by workaholic professionals who have discovered that their exciting careers are mere vanity and emptiness. This kind of questioning we could understand. But it is sometimes also secretly asked by people in Christian service careers who wonder if their preaching, counseling, and leadership is, in the end, useless and to no avail. Yet, if we take account of the book of Ecclesiastes as a whole, then it is crucial to observe that the Professor is not down on life and work as a matter of principle. On the contrary, he affirms that "A person can do nothing better than to eat and drink and find satisfaction in their own toil." In fact, he says that this positive disposition to work is "from the hand of God" (2:24). So the Professor is in a bind and, as a consequence, so are we.

Ecclesiastes and the Questioning Professor

The book of Ecclesiastes can be interpreted in one of two ways. (Ecclesiastes is the Greek translation of the Hebrew term Qoheleth in 1:1, 12 and 12:8, both Hebrew and Greek terms suggesting a community leader in the assembly, hence in English translation referred to as the Preacher or Professor.) In this book, we can understand Qoheleth as either exploring his own questions or, like an apologist, responding to questions asked by a secularist who sees life "under the sun" without faith in a transcendent God. I take the former view: the Professor is searching for "meaningful work." So the whole book could be considered an extended exposition of the curse caused by sin (Gen. 3:16-17). Taken from this perspective, life "under the sun" raises the questions: "What do workers gain from their toil" (Eccles. 3:9)? What is the result of all our efforts? What is the meaning of what we give ourselves to if there are no absolute values? As the probing Professor himself asks, "For who knows what is good for a person in life" (6:12)? And what hope do we have if there is no certain future: "Who can tell them what will happen under the sun after they are gone" (6:12)?

Surprisingly, God's word does not always come to us with packaged answers. Sometimes God lets us join an inspired author like this Professor in the very *process* of inspiration as he revels in the satisfaction of houses, programs, and pleasures but at the same time judges that all he has done is a wisp of smoke, an empty bubble. It is the same mixed feelings Christians sometimes have about work: a blessing from God, but also a curse. Work can bring great satisfaction and health to us because it takes us "out of ourselves," as Dietrich Bonhoeffer once said: "Work plunges men into the world of things. . . . The work of the world can only be done when a person forgets himself, where he loses himself in a cause."[1] And yet work can also become the idol by which we measure our own dignity. So this is our dilemma: the idol ultimately fails to deliver transcendent significance because — and here comes the kicker — we were not made for work.

The Uselessness of Work

The Professor deepens the dilemma by telling us why he thinks work is meaningless: First, it is temporary ("under the sun," 2:22). Second, your work will eventually be unappreciated ("I must leave them [my possessions] to the one who comes after me," 2:18). Third, you may give your best energies and most creative gifts to a

---

1. Dietrich Bonhoeffer, *Life Together,* trans. John W. Doberstein (New York: Harper, 1954), p. 90.

job that may subsequently be taken over by a fool ("Who knows whether that person will be wise or foolish?" 2:19). Fourth, you are certain to experience injustice in the workplace ("For a person may labor with wisdom, knowledge, and skill, and then they must leave all they own to another who has not toiled for it," 2:21). Finally, you simply must work too hard ("What do people get for all the toil and anxious striving?" 2:22). So work "under the sun" is impermanent, unappreciated, without results, unfair, and seductive.

Surprisingly, the Professor does not counsel us to cope with this situation by substituting pleasure for work. The reason is breathtaking: he is convinced that it is *God's will* for work to be useless! And God speaking through this Professor asks us to reflect on our experience of work because he wants to call us to faith in a God who has determined — ironically — that work should be useless. How can this be?

Work Becomes an Evangelist

This question about the uselessness of work that the Professor has raised probes our souls deeply. If work, even volunteer work in Christian service, proves to be meaningless, then perhaps we are being invited to conclude that we were not made for work in the first place, but rather for God. If the Professor is right, then we will not find satisfaction in our work even with the help of our faith; rather, we will find our satisfaction primarily in God in the experience of our work. It is a subtle but telling distinction.

So this deep sense of futility we share with the Professor turns out to be an inspired frustration. His holy doubt gives us the opportunity to find in God what we cannot find in our own work "under the sun." Thus work becomes an evangelist to take us to Christ. And the gospel we hear from Jesus is not that if we accept him we will be insanely happy and successful in our jobs, but that we will find our work to be satisfying "in Jesus." He alone can fill the God-shaped vacuum in our souls. So it is not just the Old Testament Professor but Jesus who asks the probing question we have been pondering. With absolute courtesy Jesus comes to us in the workplace, not to tell us what to do with our lives but to ask what meaning we are discovering in our work. And then, with infinite grace, he offers himself.[2]

For Discussion and Reflection

How do you respond to the Professor's observation that work in this life is a mixed blessing, a gift from God but also highly problematic?

In what way have you found that the frustrating dimension of your work actually points you to God?

2. Most of the foregoing appeared in R. Paul Stevens, *Seven Days of Faith: Every Day Alive to God* (Colorado Springs: Navpress, 2001), pp. 21-24.

The Wisdom Books: A Brief Summary

What are some of the important lessons we learn in these books?

First, we learn that work is intrinsically good. For that reason, it is something we should "get into" with our whole heart and not be like the sluggard in the book of Proverbs.

Second, work is an opportunity for immense creativity and entrepreneurship. It captivates us in a way that play does not, as exemplified by the entrepreneurial woman in Proverbs 31.

Third, work in this life is nonetheless enigmatic. It is a gift, a blessing, and something in which we can find satisfaction, as the Professor in Ecclesiastes shows. At the same time, it often feels futile and empty. It is at this point, therefore, just because it is so hard and fraught with problems, that work becomes a kind of evangelist — taking us back to God who alone can fill the God-shaped vacuum of our souls.

Fourth, work can occasionally be playful in itself. But God's intended counterpoise to work is a combination of play, rest, and Sabbath. These activities do not merely get us rested for the next day but are in themselves intrinsically good, bringing us a renewed perspective on the world and ourselves. While the full restoration of work and play must await the new heaven and new earth, some experience of this anticipated joy is possible even now.

Fifth, we should direct our actual work experience to God in prayer. By doing this we will discover, just as David did, that work can lead to spiritual growth and enriched ministry.

Sixth, our work, however exciting, can never be as wild, untamable, or awesome as God's work. Like Job, we discover that we are not in absolute control of the world. It follows that a full theology of work can come about only as we contemplate the incredible creativity of God.

PART FOUR

Just Work

An Introduction to the Prophets

The idea that the service to God should have only to do with a church altar, singing, reading, sacrifice, and the like is without doubt but the worst trick of the devil. How could the devil have led us more effectively astray than by the narrow conception that service to God takes place only in church and by works done therein.

Martin Luther

The rumination of the Wisdom writers, which we considered in the last part, has the force of pregnant hints and questions. Wisdom literature invites us to walk alongside someone who is reflecting, cogitating, and brooding. Compared with the Wisdom writers, the words of the prophets are like cannon blasts. The one thing that most of the prophets had in common was a passion for justice in the workplace, and they minced no words about it. Their concerns included exploited workers — concerns particularly relevant for our present information age and global business society. The workplace has not changed all that much since the days of Amos: bribery still goes on; inferior or faulty products are sold; manufactured items are misrepresented through false advertising; the poor are exploited, especially in the way resources are extracted from countries where the majority of the world lives; usurious rates of interest are charged by loan sharks who take advantage of people and companies caught in dire situations; and the gap between rich and poor yawns perilously wider. But the concerns of the prophets ring true to the present situation for another reason. They embodied the passion of God for his creatures' experience of work.

The Passion of God

In his two-volume work on the prophets, Abraham Heschel, a Jewish theologian, notes that the prophets were some of the most disturbing people who have ever lived. "The situation of a person immersed in the prophet's words," says Heschel, "is one of being exposed to a ceaseless shattering of indifference, and one needs a skull of stone to remain callous to such blows."[1] The topic is so consuming for Heschel that he devotes two volumes to probing the prophets' personalities and motivations. And it was simply this: they burned with the passion of God. They cared for what was on God's heart. Their utterances were "urging, alarming, forcing onward, as if the words gushed forth from the heart of God, seeking entrance to the heart and mind of man, carrying a summons as well as an involvement."[2] Building on the insight of Heschel, Richard Mouw coined the word "orthopathy" for this heart-gripping passion.

For the prophets, the concern for justice and righteousness was not just an impersonal thing, like the blindfolded virgin who holds the balancing scales and impartially administers justice. As Heschel says, "The style of legal, objective utterance is alien to the prophet. He dwells upon God's inner motives, not only upon His historical decisions. . . . The God of Israel is never impersonal."[3] In its fundamental meaning, the Hebrew word *mishpat* (usually translated "justice") refers to all actions that contribute to main-

1. Abraham J. Heschel, *The Prophets: An Introduction,* vol. 1 (New York: Harper & Row, 1962), p. xii.

2. Heschel, *The Prophets,* vol. 1, pp. 6-7.

3. Heschel, *The Prophets,* vol. 1, p. 24.

taining the covenant, namely the true relation between person and person, as well as between God and humankind. Therefore, it is biblically unthinkable to disassociate something like daily work from justice, that is, from doing the right thing toward others before God. So the work of the prophets, in their emotional solidarity with God, was not merely to deliver information but to deliver God's message with God's passion.

Here are some of their concerns as demonstrated by one prophet — Amos. (Others will be covered in the chapters that follow.)

Amos, Prophet of Workplace Justice

Amos prophesied about 760 B.C. during the reigns of Uzziah, king of the southern kingdom of Judah, and Jeroboam, king of the northern kingdom of Israel. Although Amos was from the south, his burden was for the north, the kingdom that had been able to take advantage of a regional power vacuum to become rich and powerful itself. This led to the emergence of a prosperous merchant class that secured for itself both winter and summer houses "adorned with ivory" (Amos 3:15). They rested on silk pillows and drank wine from bowls of gold. Merchants were tempted to increase their wealth by every means fair or foul, sometimes urged on by their consumer-oriented and slothful wives, who demanded that their husbands give them every conceivable luxury (4:1). They dined on the finest lambs, strummed their harps, and anointed themselves with the finest lotions.

All of this luxurious living on the part of the rich entailed worker exploitation, even the use of slavery. So Amos railed against workplace injustice. With red-hot passion he thundered, "They sell the innocent for silver, and the needy for [the price of] a pair of sandals" (2:6). They "deny justice to the oppressed" (2:7). They exploit the sex trade: "Father and son use the same girl" (2:7). They levy a heavy tax on the grain of the poor (5:11). They "oppress the innocent and take bribes" (5:12). Corrupt judges receive bribes and pervert justice (5:12). They use inaccurate weights and measures, "skimping on the measure, boosting the price and cheating with dishonest scales" (8:5). Some unscrupulous merchants would even sell refuse from the threshing floor: the animals treading out the grain would defecate and unscrupulous farmers would sell the waste along with the grain (8:6)!

Worse yet, all of this was given a religious coating with God-talk and Sabbath religion. The Israelite version of the current health-and-wealth gospel was reinforced from the religious centers of the land. With classic sarcasm Amos proclaimed, "Go to Bethel [the House of God] and sin" (4:4). He knew that the merchants and ruling elite had no interest in the holy day of rest anyway but used the time to plan what business deals they could pull off as soon as the Sabbath was over (8:5). No wonder Amaziah, the professional priest of Bethel in league with the exploiters, threatened to expel Amos from the land. But against all opposition, the prophet stood his ground (7:10-15).

On one hand, it appears that Amos had only bad news for the perpetrators of unfair businesses and workplaces. He compared their unjust economy to a wall about to collapse. He said that God hates religious activity that does not connect with justice in the workplace (5:21). The people would go into exile. The entire economy would collapse. The fat cats would become skinny and hungry. And worst of all, there would be a "famine of hearing the words of the LORD" (8:11). But in the midst of all this talk of judgment, Amos also offered them (and us) a positive alternative: "seek good, not evil, that you may live" (5:14).

Among the many things we learn from the life and ministry of this fiery prophet is that the gospel is not merely the gospel of personal salvation, but it is a message that has profound implications for fair wages, workers' rights, equitable interest rates, appropriate executive remuneration, reliable currency, and protection of property rights for the poor.

Did Amos see the results of his passion for justice in the workplace? We do not know. After Jeroboam's death, Israel had three kings in one year. Revolution after revolution followed and soon the Northern Kingdom was taken into captivity and the economy collapsed. But, in the meantime, Amos was expressing the heart of God by insisting on justice in the workplace and in society at large. The results of his ministry he had to leave in God's hands. Thomas Merton, writing to a young activist, said,

> Do not depend on the hope of results. When you are doing the sort of work you have taken on . . . you may have to face the fact that your work will be apparently worthless and even achieve no result at all. . . . As you get used to this idea, you start more and more to concentrate not on the result but on the value, the rightness, the truth of the work itself.[4]

In the following chapters we will consider three additional prophets: Ezekiel, who worked from his own imagination to the imagination of the people; Daniel, who worked in exile and spoke into the situation of laboring in an alien culture; and Jonah, whom we can call a reluctant missionary.

---

4. Thomas Merton, *The Hidden Ground of Love: The Letters of Thomas Merton on Religious Experience and Social Concerns,* ed. William H. Shannon (New York: Farrar, Straus and Giroux, 1985), pp. 294-97.

14

Imaginative Work — Ezekiel

*It is in the arts and the crafts that man most displays his
priestliness and historicity. . . . The painter paints because
he loves the way things look and wants to offer his sight of
them to others. The poet speaks because he loves words and
longs for them to be heard as he hears them. . . . All arts
come from having open eyes; and all arts are performing
arts. . . .*

Robert Farrar Capon, *An Offering of Uncles: The
Priesthood of Adam and the Shape of the World*

All creative work starts in the imagination. We envision something — a meal, a computer program, a piece of furniture, or a
community service program — and then we make it happen. A
cabinetmaker put it this way: "First I see the table in my mind.
Then I make a rough sketch. After this I start fashioning wood and
all the connections. At first, as it is taking shape, I think it is not as
good as I had envisioned. But when it is all done, I say, 'Beautiful!'" Can the same be said for the punch press operator, the
homecare provider, the assembly line worker, the office accoun-
tant? Yes, though perhaps in a different way. As Christian Schumacher notes, this understanding of the role of the imagination
has profound implications for the workplace: "A person cannot
reflect the Father in work unless he [or she] participates in the ac-

tual act of envisioning the object he [or she] wishes to make. That is to say the creative idea must emanate from the worker — the intuitive act of the imagination which precedes the fashioning of the actual material."[1]

Creative work and imagination are therefore inseparable. We can interpret the creation of humankind in God's own image as meaning that first we were created in God's imagination. God had a mental picture of us before putting brush to canvas, heard us as a melody before singing the song of creation, conceived us as a poem before setting down the stanzas. In short, God created *through* imagination. By the same token, God endowed humankind *with* the gift of imagination. Cheryl Forbes goes so far as to claim that "imagination is the *imago Dei* in us."[2] Whether applied in positive or negative ways (unfortunately — as we will see — we also sin in our imagination, cf. Gen. 6:5), the role of imagination is crucial in work and life. Probably no biblical character demonstrates this fact better than the prophet Ezekiel who, along with his wife, had been deported from Jerusalem to Babylon in 597 B.C.

The Prophet of the Imagination

Ezekiel exemplifies a person who goes through a major job change when war forces the economy to collapse. He was working as a priest in Jerusalem when he and thousands of others were forcibly exiled to far-away Babylon. There, by the Kebar River, the priest became a prophet, speaking God's word to his compatriots. To help him do this effectively, God gave Ezekiel visions, which Ezekiel used to inspire the people's faith through imagination. In his visions Ezekiel saw cherubim, whirling wheels, incandescent lights darting to and fro, and complex living creatures with multiple symbolic faces.

---

1. Christian Schumacher, *God in Work: Discovering the Divine Pattern for Work in the New Millennium* (Oxford: Lion, 1998), p. 75.

2. Cheryl Forbes, *Imagination: Embracing a Theology of Wonder* (Portland, Ore.: Multnomah Press, 1986), p. 18.

All of this seems initially like a very indirect way of expressing the glory of God and communicating God's purposes. But is it? Whenever God wanted to give a unique self-expression, God rarely enunciated abstract propositions; instead, the Almighty created persons who could function as visual and social metaphors of God's will. The ultimate self-expression of God, of course, came through the God-man Jesus, who in turn expressed the mystery of his identity through symbols and images such as the door, the vine, the shepherd, light, and bread.

Eastern Orthodoxy illustrates the effective use of the imagination. That tradition uses icons as an aid to worship, "windows on eternity" as they are sometimes called. As Henri Nouwen expressed it, "Whereas St. Benedict, who has set the tone for the spirituality of the West, calls us first to listen, the Byzantium fathers focus on gazing."[3] For this reason, in the words of Cheryl Forbes, "Eastern Orthodoxy comes much closer to a theology of imagination. . . . The Eastern view of worship, metaphor, and image demands that imagination play a central role in interpreting Christianity."[4] Thus, if theologians today want people to see and know God, they need to paint pictures and tell stories because, as the poet William Blake once said, we see *through* the eye into reality, perceiving its eternal, transcendent character.

Unfortunately, however, the imagination can also be used in negative ways. Although we worship God in our imagination, it is also true that we sin in the imagination, whether it is by lustful thoughts, perverted vision, twisted perceptions, soul-destroying plans, or idolatrous pictures. The people who remained in Jerusalem after the deportation were given to idolatrous and perverted imaginations. The leaders no longer led (chapter 34). The nation was a valley of dry bones (chapter 37). Ezekiel alludes to this pathetic situation in 8:12 when he describes what was going on inside the minds of the leaders left in Jerusalem. Each of them, he says, was twisted "in his chamber of imagery" (as literally trans-

3. Henri J. M. Nouwen, *Behold the Beauty of the Lord: Praying with Icons* (Notre Dame: Ave Maria Press, 1987), p. 13.

4. Forbes, *Imagination*, p. 24.

lated), or simply "in his image chamber."[5] While this could refer to a literal room full of idols, the idols or images might also be understood to exist in the minds of the leaders gathered in secrecy. At one point Ezekiel chooses the shepherd metaphor to deal with corruption in leadership. He envisages these bad leaders as feeding their own egos at the expense of the sheep (34:1-31). Sadly, the point has already made in Genesis 6:5 (cf. 12:8) that the "inclination [or "imagination" (RSV)] of the thoughts of the human heart was only evil all the time" (cf. 8:21).

So how does Ezekiel work to counter the sinful tendency in the imagination that leads to people-hurting behavior, idolatrous obsessions, and soul-numbing discouragement while he is working and living in a hostile culture? He does it by showing the people a type of video — a succession of images that would reach the head, heart, and hand through the imagination. In rapid succession Ezekiel presents a series of images, symbols, elaborate and complex creatures, colors, sounds, and movements. Through the vision of the dry bones come to life he communicates God's settled determination to renew the people (37:1-14). By the powerful final vision of God dwelling with people (43:1-12) he reminds them of their true homeland. In effect, he invites them to gaze on the beauty of God, God's grand purposes, and God's redeemed people.

Ezekiel and the Twenty-First-Century Worker

This passion for the glory of God and this appeal to our redeemed imagination gives Ezekiel's prophecies their universal and timeless quality. Like Ezekiel, we feel we are longing for our true homeland, distressed that the community that bears God's glory on earth does so in such a tawdry way, and wondering what will come of it all.[6] The word we need, as it turns out, is not so much a

---

5. As proposed by William Holladay, *Concise Hebrew and Aramaic Lexicon* (Grand Rapids: Wm. B. Eerdmans, 1971), p. 217.

6. See Walter Brueggemann, *Cadences of Home: Preaching among Exiles* (Louisville: Westminster John Knox Press, 1997).

word as a vision of the significance of the God who is absolutely determined to be glorified and known. So these visions, allegories, and parables are like the signs given to Noah long before: rainbows for a fallen world.

Our imaginations see in two different ways. In the first, the eye looks into the eternal reality and sees its true character, viewing people as image-bearers, perceiving how earth is crammed with heaven, to paraphrase the poet Elizabeth Barrett Browning.[7] But in the second way of seeing, the imagination externalizes what is inside, fleshing it out, picturing something before making it. This is surely what the artist does. And what the artist does on a grand scale in stunning relief is exactly what all workers do, to a greater or lesser extent. They see things as they are and they make things or provide a service.

It is through our imaginations that we do the most good in the world, and doing it — in all our varied human occupations — we are entering into the mind and imagination of God.[8] Thus all work can be imaginative, whether it consists of participating in a board meeting, teaching a class, delivering letters door to door, peeling potatoes, riding a bicycle, or presenting a sermon, as Ezekiel did. Part of our redemption in Christ, therefore, is the purification of our imaginations. In practical terms this involves *ascesis* — the ascetic discipline of pruning our lives of soul-numbing images from television, DVDs, the Internet, and ubiquitous advertisements. The truth is that since the Renaissance, the Industrial Revolution, and the advent of high-tech society, our lives have been largely de-imaged and stripped of imagination. On the positive side, imaginative renewal involves gazing on the beauty of God, God's purposes, and our ultimate homeland. After all, as Karl Barth said, "God is beautiful."[9]

7. Quoted in Elizabeth A. Dreyer, *Earth Crammed with Heaven: A Spirituality of Everyday Life* (New York: Paulist Press, 1994), p. 1.

8. See Robert Banks, *God the Worker: Journeys into the Mind, Heart, and Imagination of God* (Valley Forge, Pa.: Judson, 1994).

9. Karl Barth, *Dogmatics* II, 1:732-43.

For Discussion and Reflection

Recall a recent project you have undertaken. What role did your imagination have in conceiving and executing the work?

Ezekiel warned of polluting our imaginations. Reflect on the influences of distorted and sinful imaginations in your own life.

Consider what types of activities nourish imaginative health for you. What difference does each of these make to the quality of your work?

15

Exilic Work — Daniel

The Bible tells us that the Christian is in the world, and that there he or she must remain. . . . Yet we cannot deny the tension: we live in a sinful world and we cannot change it, or at least not much; at the same time we cannot accept it. . . . It is a very painful, and a very uncomfortable, situation, but it is the only position which can be fruitful for the action of the Christian in the world, and for his life in the world. . . . To be honest, this tension of the Christian must be lived.
Jacques Ellul, *The Presence of the Kingdom*

Once, I took a group of Regent College students to a local Orthodox synagogue. The rabbi insightfully commented that we are living an exilic life, even in the beautiful city of Vancouver. He was right, because we all live and work in a foreign environment, a fallen world, whether in a post-Christian, non-Christian, or anti-Christian society. Our true home is in the realm of God, which is present here and now but which will only be fully consummated in Christ at the end of history. In the meantime, we live, as some have expressed it, as "resident aliens." And it is because we, like Daniel, are "resident aliens" that the life of this prophet offers us a magnificent example of how to live and work in what are often complex and compromising situations.

Like Ezekiel, Daniel was one of the many people taken captive to Babylon by the conquering king Nebuchadnezzar. Selected as one of the cream of the crop, he was educated for three years in the wisdom and lore of the Babylonian world. This meant being immersed not only in the language of Babylon but also in its astrology, magic, and religious practices. As Joyce Baldwin notes, to study Babylonian literature was "to enter a completely different thought-world."[1] In effect, Daniel had been sent to a secular university in a foreign country. Upon "graduation," he became an agent for a pagan government. How did he cope with this?

First, Daniel compromised only in non-essentials. Although his Jewish name was Daniel, in Babylon he was given and accepted the name Belteshazzar. But when it came to essentials, including eating food prohibited for Jews, he refused to compromise. With wisdom and tact he requested a test to see whether he and his three friends would be healthier on their own vegetarian diet than on the king's food, which in fact proved to be the case. As a result of his stand, Daniel became a trusted advisor and was found to be "ten times better than all the magicians and enchanters in [Nebuchadnezzar's] whole kingdom" (Dan. 1:20).

Second, Daniel showed utter dependence on God for spiritual insight. Chapter 2 of Daniel relates the incident about the king's dream, which he kept secret yet demanded that his magicians nonetheless interpret on pain of death. When Daniel heard of the terrible decree he asked for time so that he and his three friends (now named Shadrach, Meshach, and Abednego) could pray to God for insight into the meaning of the dream. After God revealed the dream to Daniel, he said to the king, "There is a God in heaven who reveals mysteries. He has shown King Nebuchadnezzar what will happen in days to come" (2:28). Then Daniel proceeded to explain that the king's vision was about the passing of realms, starting with Babylon but ending with the one that will be everlasting, the realm of God. In this way Daniel showed that history is going somewhere, has a goal and purpose, and that its unfolding is under the gracious and saving rule of God — an in-

---

1. Joyce Baldwin, *Daniel: An Introduction and Commentary* (Downers Grove, Ill.: InterVarsity Press, 1978), p. 80.

sight into the future that Daniel could only have received from God alone.

Third, Daniel believed in the power of God. As is well known, Daniel's three friends were thrown into a fiery furnace for refusing to worship the image of the king. But before being put in the furnace they declared to the king, "The God we serve is able to deliver us from it, and he will deliver us from Your Majesty's hand. But even if he does not, we want you to know, Your Majesty, that we will not serve your gods or worship the image of gold you have set up" (3:17-18). In anger the king ordered the furnace to be heated seven times hotter than usual, but when he looked up, to his amazement he saw a fourth person in the furnace, one who looked like "a son of the gods." Miraculously, the three men emerged unharmed from the furnace — an extraordinary testimony to faith and the power of God to deliver.

Fourth, Daniel modeled competence and integrity in the workplace. The incident that eventually led up to Daniel being cast into the lions' den (chapter 6) highlights Daniel's personal integrity and administrative competence. During the reign of King Darius, Daniel was one of three chief administrators in the land. But Daniel was no ordinary administrator. In fact, he "so distinguished himself among the administrators and the satraps by his exceptional qualities that the king planned to set him over the whole kingdom" (6:3). Jealous of this proposed promotion, the other administrators and the satraps "tried to find grounds for charges against Daniel in his conduct of government affairs, but they were unable to do so. They could find no corruption in him, because he was trustworthy and neither corrupt nor negligent" (6:4-5). What we see in Daniel, therefore, is a man who throughout his life, from beginning to end (cf. 1:20), practiced excellence and integrity in the workplace.

Fifth, Daniel's life-giving patterns of spiritual discipline sustained him. In addition to demonstrating Daniel's personal integrity, the incident of the lions' den also speaks volumes about his pattern of spiritual discipline. Clearly, it consisted not just of occasional fasting but of daily and regular prayer. Three times a day Daniel and his friends faced Jerusalem and prayed. It is interesting to observe, however, that it was this practice that also got them into trouble with the Babylonian bureaucracy. Since the other administrators could not find fault with Daniel's job performance, they attacked his religion. By having the king pass a law that in the next thirty days any person who prayed to any god other than the king would be thrown into the lions' den, Daniel's enemies were determined to get him this time. And, sure enough, because Daniel insisted on maintaining his discipline of daily prayer, he was thrown into the den, even though the king was distressed about it and wanted to rescue him. In the end, to the king's delight, Daniel eventually emerged from the den safe and unharmed, thus giving powerful witness to the importance of maintaining spiritual disciplines at all costs.

Daniel and the Modern Workplace

Daniel's life teaches us many things about how to both survive and thrive in the workplace. For one thing, he shows us that compromise on nonessentials is sometimes inevitable when working in Babylon and other "exilic" countries, though one must also know how to discern the difference between the essentials and nonessentials. Daniel was an expert at this. Early Christians faced a similar challenge when the Caesar cult demanded the pinch of incense in honor of the Roman emperor along with the confession, "Caesar is Lord," in contradistinction to their Christian confession that "Jesus is Lord." Years ago during the international exhibition "Expo 67" in Montreal when I was entertaining leaders from the church in communist Russia, long before the Berlin wall came down, I asked how they functioned in a corrupt and totalitarian system such as communism. "No human system or kingdom is eternal," they said. In the same way, Daniel's example affirms for us the appropriateness of attending a public university and taking up a government service position even if the government is corrupt.

At the same time, the story of Daniel's life shows us the importance of practicing excellence in the work we do. As Dorothy

Sayers says, the first duty his religion gives a carpenter is that he should make good tables. The story is also told of St. Augustine, who was criticized for buying his sandals from non-Christian sandal-makers. To this complaint he is reported to have replied, "I do too much walking to walk on inferior sandals." This does not necessarily mean that all Christian sandal-makers did shoddy work, but that in this case Augustine preferred a pair of sandals from a non-Christian artisan because of their superior quality. Daniel was nothing if not an excellent worker.

Along with competence and excellence, Daniel's life demonstrates the importance of maintaining one's spiritual disciplines and integrity in the workplace. This kind of example helps us speak to the evil and sins of the workplace and to call people to the highest standard. Of course, such speaking must be done with much discretion. Daniel did not go around saying, "I am a worshiper of Yahweh and you people are going to hell for worshiping the king and bowing down to his image." He waited for the right moment to say, "There is a God in heaven who reveals mysteries" (Dan. 2:28). And we too will find that there is a right moment to say, "Jesus is Lord." In this way our very work life becomes a witness that is communicated both verbally and nonverbally.

For Discussion and Reflection

What are the compromises you have made as you work "in exile"? Were they in nonessentials or essentials? How is it possible, if it is, to compromise faithfully?

In what way has the story of Daniel given you practical help to live and work in complicated circumstances that are not faith-reinforcing?

The dramatic incidents recorded in the book of Daniel were spread over a lifetime with long spaces between events. What can this teach you about working as a witness even when people are not asking you to tell them about your God?

16

Missionary Work — Jonah

Anger is a most useful diagnostic tool. When anger erupts within us, it is a signal that something is wrong. . . . What [Jonah's anger] reveals is an immature imagination, an undeveloped vocation. His wrong was not in his head but in his heart.

Eugene Peterson, *Under the Unpredictable Plant:*
An Exploration in Vocational Holiness

The book of Jonah — one of the so-called Minor Prophets — can best be thought of as a prophetic comedy. Its ultimate purpose is to get God's reluctant witnesses then and now to laugh their way into genuine mission. Good humor is an act of worship because it is an admission of creatureliness and an implicit recognition that we are not God. By contrast, anger is often evoked by the frustration people feel when they cannot control God or their world. And this is the situation in which our main character in this Old Testament book finds himself: he is too angry to laugh. Instead of responding with gratitude to a nation-wide repentance that was the epitome of his prophetic career, "to Jonah this seemed very

---

This chapter is adapted from R. Paul Stevens, *Seven Days of Faith: Every Day Alive to God*, chapter 18 (Colorado Springs: Navpress, 2001), pp. 193-200.

wrong, and he became angry" (Jonah 4:1). God's last question in the book — "Do you have the right to be angry?" (4:9, CEV) — is intended to probe Jonah's paralyzed spirituality with words that could lead to the birth of faith, hope, and love.

The book of Jonah describes a form of work to which all believers are called, some as leaders of congregations or missionaries crossing cultural frontiers, and others, meaning most of us, as persons who are called to be witnesses in the context of our daily lives and work. But this book probes our hearts deeply to expose the *real* reason why we are sometimes reluctant to share the good news with people different from us. It also explores the way missionaries are spiritually formed in the process of doing their work. Ironically, God's spiritual agenda is accomplished by a strategy strangely at odds with modern agencies that send out missionaries: God calls an angry man to share a message he hardly believes, with people he does not like, in order that the missionary himself might be saved! Thus this story becomes a paradigm for people called to be evangelists, but who themselves need to be evangelized.

The Archetypical Reluctant Witness

God called Jonah to evangelize the city of Nineveh, the capital of the Assyrian superpower threatening Israel at the time. Instead of traveling 750 miles east across the desert to Nineveh, Jonah took to the sea and headed in the opposite direction to Tarshish (Spain), thus putting distance between the call of God and himself. But Jonah was soon to discover that he could not easily escape God's call. In the event, God sent a violent storm that prompted everyone on board to cry out to their gods, everyone except Jonah, because he was asleep in the hull soothing his conscience. When the sailors realized that their present crisis was an embodiment of the storm inside Jonah, they pried out the identity of this reluctant missionary with their insistent questions, "What do you do? Where do you come from? . . . From what people are you?" (1:8).

Jonah told them that he worshiped the God who made the sea, that he was running away from that God, and that nothing would calm the storm except the sacrifice of the missionary. He urged them to throw him overboard. Instead, trying — unsuccessfully — to row back to land in the face of the storm (1:13), these pagan sailors risked their own lives to save the life of God's reluctant servant. (Sometimes, people who don't know God show more love than the people who do.) After much agonizing, the sailors finally heeded his request and threw him overboard. Amazingly, the sea grew calm, causing the pagan sailors to convert to Jonah's God and offer sacrifices to the Lord. A revival on board the ship!

Converting the Missionary

Meanwhile, Jonah was swallowed by a great fish and remained inside its belly for three days and three nights, oblivious to what was happening on board the ship. With hilarious irony, enough to make anyone howl with laughter, the narrator shows that in fact the missionary got dumped and the pagans got saved! Sometimes, people who don't know God show more faith than the people who do.

But inside the great fish, Jonah did not laugh; instead he prayed for the first time in the story (2:1-9). Jonah had achieved his wish to be separated from God, but it was in that very separation that he *found* God. No wonder Jonah's prayer in the belly of the fish became altogether unselfish: he had found grace in the midst of divine judgment. He now knew that God was *for* him. Therefore he gave thanks and made no further petitions. Jonah was making progress; he was now an almost-saved missionary.

Trying again with Jonah, God made the great fish vomit the reluctant missionary onto the beach and then called him a second time. This time Jonah obeyed because he understood that God meant business both with him and with the rest of God's covenant people who had no missionary vision. Yet, when he finally made his way to Nineveh, the prophet still did not believe God meant to redeem those outside God's chosen people. Therefore, he preached a doomsday message while walking up and down the streets of the great city, not realizing that God's judgment is always laced with hope. Ironically, the Ninevites and their king intuitively understood this better than Jonah did. So the king issued a proclamation in the hope that "God may yet relent and with compassion turn from his fierce anger" (3:9). Sometimes people who don't know God have more hope than the people who do. But perhaps the supreme irony in the story is that it was easier for *God* to stop being angry than for the missionary to do so — as vividly illustrated in the next incident.

When Jonah saw that God's mind had changed about Nineveh, he decided to change his own mind about serving God. As a last desperate attempt to defend his ethnocentric theology, Jonah bitterly complained about the wideness of mercy in God's heart: "I knew that you are a gracious and compassionate God" (4:2). All along he had been afraid that he would not be able to control God's response to his preaching, that God would be too soft on Israel's enemies. After all, God's anger was not "pure" like his own. Grace bothered him. Unfortunately, Jonah would not make his peace with the grace of God until the death and resurrection he had experienced in the whale was matched by a corresponding death and resurrection in his own heart.

Still hoping to see doom and damnation visited on the Ninevites, Jonah camped outside the city to see what would happen, much as a geologist might camp beside a volcano hoping it would erupt while he was watching. But God was not about to humor the prophet's callous heart. Instead, God first provided a vine to give shade for Jonah in the heat of the day but then sent a worm to attack the vine leaving Jonah exposed to the scorching sun, showing that God will go to almost any lengths to bring a person back. It's as though God were saying, "If the whale doesn't work, perhaps the worm will." But it turned out that Jonah's interaction with the worm revealed more of his inner attitude than his experience with the whale. The worm showed that Jonah still cared for no one but himself. Jonah lived for his own righteousness, his own theology, and his own ministry. But he was quickly being stripped of all these possessions. Already having lost his honor as a messenger of the wrath of God, he now lost his creature comforts.

Sulking outside the city, Jonah wallowed in his anger, self-pity, and self-righteousness. When God asked the probing question, "Is it right for you to be angry?" Jonah persisted in defending himself: "I'm so angry I wish I were dead" (4:9). What, after all, is the point of living if God will not do what Jonah expects? What is the point of being a missionary if grace is unpredictable? What is the point of being in ministry if God cannot be controlled?

Losing Control of God

We are not told how the story ends. Instead we are left with a question from God that invites us to supply our own ending, to put ourselves into the story: "You have been concerned about this plant. . . . Should I not have concern for the great city of Nineveh?" (4:10-11). The book of Jonah calls us to let God be God. And it powerfully suggests that if we do not, God will still be God and will continue to love the outsiders for whom we have no love. This prophetic comedy reveals that we have a God who will convert pagans when they throw believers overboard, a God who will vomit believing workers out of their own private hells and send them into service a second time. In doing so God sends them to serve people who will convince the messengers of their own message. If we hear the story of Jonah and are silent, even the stones might laugh.

This book is not about a big fish but about a big God. The book does not invite us to muster enough faith to believe that God could arrange to have a person swallowed and vomited by a big fish, but to have the greater faith that God could capture us reluctant missionaries for something larger than we dreamed: the renewal of the entire world in the Messiah, Jesus. Jonah offers a case study in missionary spirituality, not just for one reluctant prophet and his Old Testament contemporaries in 750 B.C., but for all gospel-hoarders at home or on the mission field today. If we do not recognize that our anger paralyzes authentic mission, God, out of unconditional love for us, may have to use pagans to break up our stony hearts. Better to double up in repentant laughter now.

Once I was too tired to witness, and as I slumped into the seat for a long bus ride to a distant city I said to the Lord, "No witnessing today, please!" A long-haired rock singer sat beside me to make his way to a singing engagement in the same city. He refused to be impressed with my closed eyes and my icy silence.

> "What do you do?" he asked.
> "I teach."
> "What do you teach?"
> "I teach about God," I replied with as little enthusiasm as possible.
> "Oh, that's interesting. Tell me more. . . . Do you know God? What is he like?"

My name is Jonah.

For Discussion and Reflection

We have noted the missing ending to this story. How would you write the ending for yourself?

When, if ever, have you been evangelized by the very people you thought you had been sent to evangelize?

In what way do you think "mission work" is something to which all followers of Christ are called?

Have you ever been angry at God? What do you now understand was the source of that anger?

The Prophetic Books: A Brief Summary

What are some of the things we learn from the prophetic books?

First, we learn that God is passionately concerned about how we work and the effect of human work on other people, societies, and the environment. The same passion that gripped the hearts of the prophets can grip all workers who line themselves up with God's interests.

Second, good work is characterized by justice, giving what is due to the worker and the neighbor. The opposite of just work is any form of enterprise that exploits, abuses, manipulates, and harms people and places. Such work is to be avoided at all costs.

Third, work must be understood not only in terms of its outward results but also in relation to the imagination from which those results flow. Good work comes from a good inner life.

Fourth, most Christians today work in a pluralistic and frequently compromising culture. Rather than keeping faith and work in separate compartments, or simply conforming to the surrounding secularism, the example of Daniel invites us to a thoroughgoing integration of faith and work. While some form of compromise in nonessentials is inevitable in such "exilic" situations, it is nonetheless possible, albeit with attendant risks and challenges, to work with integrity.

Fifth, while some people are specifically called to cross major cultural frontiers to share the gospel of the kingdom of God, all believers are providentially sent by God into workplaces as missionaries. In these workplaces, we bear witness both by deed and word. Moreover, the work we do should not be regarded simply as a means for gaining access to the universal "mission field" of the workplace; rather, the work itself is part of God's mission on earth, in which we participate. This will become even more clear in the next few studies.

PART FIVE

Kingdom Work

An Introduction to the New Testament

Any job that serves humanity and in which one can glorify God is a Kingdom job.

Leland Ryken, *Work and Leisure*
in Christian Perspective

As we open the New Testament we find God in-the-flesh at work in the world. The four Good News books, or Gospels, were a unique literary creation to introduce people to the life, teaching, and deeds of Jesus and the extraordinary message he embodied — *the gospel of the kingdom of God.* But it is a remarkable truth that this God in-the-flesh was born to a young peasant girl and then apprenticed to his father as a carpenter who, according to tradition, made plows and yokes. Notice that long before Jesus had preached a sermon or worked a miracle he had sawed and sanded wood for a couple of decades, made cradles and tables, and dealt with customers both kind and ornery. This is the Son with whom God was "well pleased" (Matt. 3:17).

But Jesus was not only a tradesperson; he could also be thought of as an entrepreneur for God's realm, calling the twelve disciples, sending out the seventy, teaching the crowd, healing many people, and ministering to their emotional, psychological, and physical needs. His choosing twelve ordinary, working individuals, not professional clergy, as his closest associates shows that

Jesus' work was not that of a religious professional. His associates included four fishermen as well as people of questionable professions such as a tax collector and a zealot (read "insurgent"). Of Jesus' 132 public appearances in the New Testament, 122 were in the marketplace; of the fifty-two parables that Jesus told, forty-five had a workplace context. No wonder Jesus could say, "My Father is always at his work to this very day, and I too am working" (John 5:17). And the book of Acts, which begins the next section of the New Testament canon, could well be called the works that Jesus continued to do through the Spirit in the apostles (Acts 1:1). Here again the workplace figures prominently: of forty divine interventions recorded in that book, thirty-nine took place in the marketplace or public square!

Similarly, the section of letters in the New Testament contains a great deal about work. For instance, in two of his earliest letters, if not *the* earliest letters, namely 1 and 2 Thessalonians, Paul had to confront the serious problem in the church of people refusing to work in anticipation of the Lord's return (2 Thess. 3:6-13). Paul urged these people to "work with your hands," just as he had previously told them (1 Thess. 4:11). Then, in two of his later letters, those to the Ephesians and the Colossians, he devotes major sections to what are called "house tables" (cf. Eph. 5:21–6:9; Col. 3:18–4:1), so called because they deal with household matters, remembering, however, that a "household" in Greco-Roman society often included the workplace. Hence to the slaves in Colossae he said, "*Whatever you do,* work at it with all your heart, as working for the Lord, not for human masters, since you know that you will receive an inheritance from the Lord as a reward. It is the Lord Christ you are serving" (Col. 3:23-24). This statement may be compared with his general instruction to the whole church, "*Whatever you do,* whether in word or deed, do it all in the name of the Lord Jesus" (Col. 3:17). In addition, the apostolic letters give positive reasons for engaging in work, such as supplying one's own needs instead of being dependent on others and thereby winning "the respect of outsiders" as a witness (1 Thess. 4:11-12), as well as enabling a person to give to others in need (Eph. 4:28).

Finally, in the very last book of the Bible, the Revelation, John envisages the new heaven and new earth along with the marriage supper of the Lamb. And surprisingly, as we will see, our final destiny is not a workless utopia but a renewed world in which we will work with infinite creativity and fulfillment. In that place, there will be no more curse. So who would not want to go to such a heaven? But there we will not be disembodied spirits or mere "saved souls." Instead, in that new heaven *and new earth* we anticipate being fully resurrected persons (body, soul, and spirit), since the visions of the new heaven and the new earth are given in terms of what we know and do now (Rev. 21:22-27). In fact, the final vision of the Bible is that of "the Holy City, the new Jerusalem, *coming down out of heaven*" (21:2) to take up residence here. In one sense, therefore, our environment is going to heaven, as are our culture, our government, our crafts, and our work. Earth is now crammed with heaven, as one book title suggests,[1] but the reverse is also true: heaven is crammed with earth.

The Gospel of the Kingdom

If Jesus was an entrepreneur in any sense, what enterprise was he building? The answer to that question is in no doubt: it was the realm of God. From the beginning of his ministry (Mark 1:15) to the end (Acts 1:3), his driving passion was to declare the coming of the kingdom, God's kingdom. Many people think that Jesus' main message was to proclaim the gospel of personal salvation, but his own words reveal a perspective much bigger and broader than that. While it is true that a relationship with Jesus brings people into new birth and renewal of life, his kingdom theology — that is, his proclamation of the rule of God — reaches far beyond soul salvation. According to Jesus' teaching, the kingdom is the dynamic saving and renewing rule of God in people and creation and, as we shall soon see, even in work.

---

1. Elizabeth Dreyer, *Earth Crammed with Heaven: A Spirituality of Everyday Life* (New York: Paulist, 1994).

But if we wonder what this realm is like, we need look no further than Jesus himself. One father of the church has rightly called Jesus the *autobasileia,* a Greek word that means God's realm in Jesus' own person. We can see this being lived out in Jesus' ministry of healing the sick, feeding the multitudes, comforting the poor and destitute, speaking hope and forgiveness to all through his death on the cross and resurrection from the grave. Jesus' message about the kingdom is holistic and not just spiritual. God's realm is personal, social, political, economic, and cosmic. In other words, the coming of God's realm would have profound and far-reaching implications for all spheres of life, which has been eloquently articulated by a number of recent writers.

For instance, the Mennonite writer John Howard Yoder expressed it this way: "Jesus was not just a moralist whose teachings had some political implications; he was not primarily a teacher of spirituality. . . ." Rather, Jesus was "the bearer of a new possibility of human, social, and therefore political relationships."[2]

Along the same lines, Andrew Crouch writes concerning Jesus' realm:

[His] good news foretold a comprehensive restructuring of social life comparable to that experienced by a people when one monarch was succeeded by another. The kingdom of God would touch every sphere and every scale of culture. It would reshape marriage and mealtimes, resistance to the Roman occupiers and prayer in the temple, the social standing of prostitutes and the piety of Pharisees, the meaning of cleanliness and the interpretation of illness, integrity in business and honesty in prayer.[3]

The South American theologian Mortimer Arias goes even further in identifying the disturbing presence of God's realm in the world and in the church:

2. John H. Yoder, *The Politics of Jesus* (Grand Rapids: Eerdmans, 1972), p. 63.

3. Andrew Crouch, *Culture Making: Recovering Our Creative Calling* (Downers Grove, Ill.: InterVarsity Press, 2008), p. 138, quoted in Ben Witherington III, *Work: A Kingdom Perspective on Labor* (Grand Rapids: Eerdmans, 2011), p. 112.

The coming of the kingdom means a permanent confrontation of worlds. . . . [It means] an irreverent exposure of human motivations and of the most sacred rules of human mores. The kingdom is an iconoclastic disturber of religious sacred places and customs. . . . [It] is the appointed challenger of all sacralizing myths and systems and the relentless unmasker of all human disguises, self-righteous ideologies, or self-perpetuating powers.[4]

So what has all this to do with work?

Kingdom Work

Since the scope of redemption in Christ is the same as the scope of creation, therefore work is done for God's realm when it creates new wealth, alleviates poverty, brings well-being to people, reconciles people to God, embellishes and improves human life, sometimes even in conflict with powers resistant to God's coming *shalom*. This means that doctors, mechanics, technicians, homemakers, politicians, pastors, evangelists, school teachers, nurses, artists, musicians, farmers, scientists, businesspeople, counselors, laborers — all do kingdom work when they serve God's purposes in bringing renewal and development to God's creation. It also means that some people are doing the work of God's realm without knowing God and without knowing that they are doing God's work.

Calvin Seerveld tells a moving story from his childhood that illustrates the mystery of working in God's realm. "My father is a seller of fish," he says. "[But in reality he] is in full-time service for the Lord, prophet, priest, and king in the fish business. And customers who come into the store sense it. . . . [That] little Great South Bay Fish Market . . . is not only a clean, honest place where you can buy quality fish at a reasonable price with a smile, but

4. Mortimer Arias, *Announcing the Reign of God: Evangelization and the Subversive Memory of Jesus* (Lima, Ohio: Academic Renewal Press, 1984), pp. 46-47.

there is a spirit in the store, a spirit of laughter, of fun, joy inside the buying and selling that strikes the observer pleasantly."[5]

Ideally, all work should express itself in that kind of devotion to excellence and *joie de vivre* — even if it represents only an ideal to strive for. Yet when Paul wrote to the Thessalonians, he commended them for being a people whose "labor [was] *prompted by love*" (1 Thess. 1:3). Admittedly, not everyone loves his or her work, but love can turn even a routine job into a ministry by finding new ways to accomplish an old task or doing something with the extra flair that love inspires. Embellishment is one of the love-works that make the daily round interesting and at least create a potential for ministry. When I first reflected on this I was staying in a guest house in a tiny Moslem village on the Indian Ocean in Kenya. Most of the people were very, very poor, yet almost every wooden doorpost and lintel was rendered beautiful and interesting by exquisite Swahili carvings, each design unique. Such attention to detail requires effort, the effort that love makes.

Work provides opportunities for loving our neighbors as ourselves (Matt. 22:39). While there are obviously some jobs that do not qualify in this regard (prostitution and drug-pushing would be prime examples), I think the list is shorter than some would imagine. Much more complicated is the range of jobs in the "gray areas" — jobs in which some people in the marketplace engage: being a stock broker or a collections agent who sells people's furniture from under them. Can these be done for love? Does the politician's work allow for love, or the work of a revolutionary, a soldier, an executioner, or an ambassador for a corrupt government? Someone working in the advertising field may be obliged, from time to time, to sell things by sex. Can he or she work for this firm for love? An international buyer will find that success sometimes requires kickbacks, a complicated challenge that is viewed very differently in other cultures. Is there a place for love in such a business? We see that defining the work of God's realm can be a

---

5. Calvin Seerveld, *Christian Workers Unite!* (Toronto: Christian Labour Association of Canada [90 Hadrian Drive, Rexdale, Ontario], 1964), pp. 7-8. Quoted with permission.

tricky business. But our business is not to define, but to do whatever work falls into our hands "with all [our] heart, as working for the Lord, not for human masters" (Col. 3:23). In this way, we will discover that even ordinary work in the world can last into eternity, or to put it another way, can have eternity folded into it.

If it is true that all human work that embodies God's values and serves God's goals is rightly called God's work, then it follows that the old distinction between sacred work and so-called secular work can no longer be maintained. The two are actually interdependent and necessary. The book of Acts gives an evocative description of Paul, Priscilla, and Aquila working to sew canvas tents together to support their ministry of church-planting and discipleship. For Aquila and Priscilla tent-making apparently was full-time work; for Paul it was part-time. Either way, the work was of equal value. These are some of the lessons we will learn in the next few chapters.

17

Contemplative Work — Martha

Without the opportunity to learn through the hands, the world remains abstract, and distant, and the passions for learning will not be engaged.

Doug Stowe, quoted in Matthew B. Crawford, *Shop Class as Soul Craft: An Inquiry into the Value of Work*

Unfortunately, one of the characters in the New Testament, a manual worker, has received a lot of bad press. People consider Martha, a friend of Jesus, absurdly busy, occupied with such mundane physical things as meals, beds, and swept floors, while Mary, her sister, the model saint, sits at the feet of Jesus and absorbs every word in contemplation. The story is briefly told in Luke 10:38-42.

Not surprisingly, this story has been the subject of much reflection and controversy throughout the history of the church. Some have seen it simply as two personality types, one more active than the other: extrovert and introvert. Others have seen this as the root of various religious orders and para-church organizations, some of which are given to the contemplative life, such as the Benedictines, while others, like the Franciscans and Protestant mission societies, are committed to the active life. Still other people — and this is the most common interpretation — have seen the incident as the Lord's affirmation of the superiority of the religious life — whether pastor, missionary, priest, nun, or monk — over ordinary life in the world. So the church has a long tradition of exalting the religious vocation over domestic life, marriage and family, the household world of pots and pans, swept floors, the offer of generous hospitality, and engagement in practical work.

The early historian Eusebius of Caesarea in his *Demonstration of the Gospel* (A.D. 312) compared these two ways. Quoting Philo, Eusebius notes that the superior way involves the abandonment of property. These believers have said "farewell to all the cares of life" and now make their dwelling in deserts and oases. They abandon trade and marriage. "Having laid down for the soul continence as a foundation, they build the other virtues on it." The women pay "no attention to bodily pleasures, longing not for mortal but for immortal children."[1]

In this way Eusebius gave endorsement to the dualism that has characterized the church for twenty centuries, namely, the idea that pastors and priests do holy work while ordinary people in the home, on the worksite, or in business do secular work.[2] Saint Augustine (354-430) reinforced this notion by saying that although both action and contemplation were needed, "it is contemplation, nevertheless, which lays particular claim to the office of investigating the nature of truth."[3]

Yet, a closer look at the passage in question suggests that a much less polarized interpretation of the Martha/Mary narrative is not only possible but necessary. As Luke tells the story, the disciples and Jesus were enjoying an "evening out" with their special friends Mary, Martha, and probably also Lazarus. It was Martha's home and, as hostess, she was busy with "all the preparations that

---

1. *Eusebius: The Ecclesiastical History*, trans. Kirsopp Lake (Cambridge, Mass.: Harvard University Press, 1953), Vol. 1, II, xvii, pp. 147, 153.

2. See Mark Greene, *The Great Divide* (London: The London Institute for Contemporary Christianity, 2010).

3. Quoted in Bruce Hindmarsh, "Vita Activa or Vita Contemplativa? A Mixed Life or a Mixed Up Life? Spiritual Theology, Spiritual Disciplines for the Marketplace," Knoxville, Tenn., Regent Marketplace Institute, May 2004 (unpublished), p. 2.

had to be made," while Mary "sat at the Lord's feet listening to what he said." Now, we may well ask, What was so wrong with Martha providing hospitality for Jesus and his friends? Not much. Or, What was so right about Mary's inaction, letting Martha do all the work? Not much, either. But what we will see is that there was in fact something wrong with Martha (her attitude), and there was something right about Mary (her devotion).

As for Martha, she felt overcommitted, obsessed as she was with all the preparations. "Few things are needed," Jesus said (v. 42). Thoughtlessly Martha blamed the Lord. "Don't you care?" she asked, trying to "triangle" Jesus to get some help. "Tell her to help me," she demanded (v. 40), and thereby spoiled the party for Jesus, for the disciples, and for herself. Sadly, Martha had neglected what Jesus most wanted — fellowship. As for Mary, what she had done right was to sit at Jesus' feet to receive the blessing of his ministry, one of the few things really necessary in life (v. 42). Yet if only Martha and Mary had understood that it was not a case of doing one or the other, but in fact of doing both, the altercation may never have happened.

The History of Mary and Martha

What is remarkable as we read the Gospels is that Jesus in his life on earth combined the roles of Mary and Martha. At times he was so engaged in practical service that he could not eat. But on other occasions he withdrew to the mountain alone to pray, on one such occasion even having to dismiss the crowd and tell them to go home so that he could continue praying. So in spite of the polarization throughout much of church history over the active versus the contemplative life, it is gratifying to note that the best of church tradition actually does combine Mary and Martha as parallel patterns for Christian living.

We see this, for instance, in the way Walter Hilton, a twelfth-century Augustinian Christian, responded to a businessman who considered leaving commerce to become a monk by suggesting the alternative: combine action and contemplation.

You ought to mingle the works of an active life with spiritual endeavors of a contemplative life, and then you will do well. For you should at certain times be busy with Martha in the ordering and care of your household, children, employees, tenants, or neighbors. . . . At other times you should, with Mary, leave off the busyness of this world and sit down meekly at the feet of our Lord, there to be in prayer, holy thought, and contemplation of him, as he gives you grace. . . . In so doing, you will be keeping well the order of charitable love.[4]

Teresa of Avila (1515-1582), the leader of a renewal movement within a monastic order, called for a parallel lifestyle by urging Mary to be more helpful to Martha:

Believe me, Martha and Mary must join together in order to show hospitality to the Lord and have Him always present and not host Him badly by failing to give Him something to eat. How would Mary, always seated at His feet, provide Him with food if her sister did not help her?[5]

On the other hand, Francis de Sales (1567-1622), in his advice to an ordinary non-religious woman, commended the "mixed life" by urging that action be perfected by contemplation:

No, Philothea, true devotion does us no harm whatsoever, but instead perfects all things. . . . Every vocation becomes more agreeable when united with devotion. Care of one's family is rendered more peaceable, love of husband and wife more sincere, service to one's principle more faithful, and every type of employment more pleasant and agreeable. It is an error, or rather a heresy, to wish to banish the devout life from the regi-

---

4. Walter Hilton, *Toward a Perfect Love,* trans. David L. Jeffrey (Portland, Ore.: Multnomah Press, 1985), pp. 8-9.

5. Teresa of Avila, *Interior Castle,* trans. E. Allison Peers (New York: Doubleday, 1989), p. 231.

ment of soldiers, the mechanic's shop, the court of princes, or the home of married people.[6]

What all these people are saying, then, is that we can have neither action without contemplation nor contemplation without action. Like horse and carriage, love and marriage, they belong together.

In conclusion, here are three things to reflect on in relation to work.

First, manual work is good work, even holy work. Physical work in the carpenter's shop, on the construction site, in the home or factory, on farms and on city streets, is not only good work but godlike work. It is work that engages our minds and hearts. Through it we can learn just as much as we might learn in knowledge work as teachers, professors, and pastors. As David Crawford says in *Shop Class as Soul Craft,* "Every trade . . . offers its own intrinsic satisfactions, characteristic frustrations, and cognitive challenges; sometimes the challenges are rich enough to be totally absorbing."[7] Much of the work we do can actually inspire contemplation and reflection.

Second, no work should be so all-absorbing that it prevents reflection and prayer. The story of Martha and Mary shows us that we need to be people involved in active contemplation. Opportunities for such active contemplation can arise in the midst of a busy workday. For instance, repetitive work provides almost endless opportunities for prayer, even while scrubbing floors in the home with children tugging at your pant legs. In his book *The Practice of the Presence of God,* Brother Lawrence said that his many duties were not allowed to divert him from God. Even in the monastery kitchen with the clatter of pots and pans all around, Lawrence found time to meditate. And always before undertaking some special assignment he would pray, "Lord, I can-

6. Francis de Sales, *Introduction to a Devout Life,* ed. Thomas S. Kepler (New York: The World Publishing Company, 1952), p. 33.

7. Matthew B. Crawford, *Shop Class as Soul Craft: An Inquiry into the Value of Work* (New York: Penguin Press, 2009), p. 36.

not do this unless Thou enablest me."[8] I myself have found that before beginning a task such as cutting an expensive piece of California redwood or meeting with a business client, it is a good idea to pray.

Third, being an active contemplative today involves taking the initiative. Modern life does not permit much down time, yet most of us need a rhythm of action and withdrawal. The problem today is that we fill even domestic work with noise such as cell phones, iPods, and continuous music. Even in our cars going to the grocery store or to the construction site, we have lost a few minutes of solitude by turning on the radio, CD player, or our hands-free cell phones. All of this makes it very hard to pursue the example of Mary and Martha at the same time. So what can be done? We have to discipline ourselves to exploit the opportunities that exist for contemplation. We need to look on routine and manual work, whether filing things in the home office or cutting the lawn, as a gift. And of course going to the park or coffee shop or sitting in an empty church or withdrawing into our "closets" can provide wonderful opportunities for meditation and sitting quietly like Mary at Jesus' feet. But then we must also get up to do the work of Martha.

As Archbishop of Westminster Basil Hume once said, "No man can afford to live in the marketplace who does not also live in the desert." For us this means that every Christian should have the hyphenated name of Mary-Martha.

For Discussion and Reflection

Discuss the following quotation by Alain de Botton: "How different everything is for the craftsman who transforms a part of the world with his own hands, who can see his work as emanating from his being and can step back at the end of the day or lifetime and point to an object — whether a square of canvas, a chair, or a

---

8. Brother Lawrence, *The Practice of the Presence of God* (Westwood, N.J.: Fleming H. Revell, 1958), pp. 17, 19.

clay jug — and see it as a stable repository of his skills."[9] Do you agree or disagree with this evaluation of manual work? Why or why not?

Even if you earn your living in knowledge or IT work, glued to a computer screen, or in any other occupation that does not demand physical labor, some of your work, whether in the woodshop, kitchen, or backyard, whether remunerated or not, is manual. What have you learned about yourself through that work?

9. Alain de Botton, *The Pleasures and Sorrows of Work* (New York: Pantheon Books, 2009), p. 182.

18

Tent-making Work — Paul, Aquila, and Priscilla

The priesthood of all believers did not make everyone into church workers; rather it turned every kind of work into a sacred calling.

Gene E. Veith

The tent-making model — in which a person would have two arenas in which to serve God, the workplace and the church — was the form of church leadership that dominated the first three centuries of the church's history, as explained in Roland Allen's important book, *The Case for the Voluntary Clergy*.[1] The New Testament has different examples of such tentmakers, the most striking of which are the apostle Paul and his close friends, Aquila and Priscilla.

Full-Time and Part-Time Tentmakers

From the beginning of his missionary career Paul combined preaching the gospel with practical work, as indicated in two of his earliest letters, 1 and 2 Thessalonians. Speaking autobiographi-

---

1. Roland Allen, *The Case for the Voluntary Clergy* (London: Eyre & Spottiswoode, 1930).

cally in his first letter to the church in Thessalonica, Paul wrote, "Surely you remember, brothers and sisters, our toil and hardship; we worked night and day in order not to be a burden to anyone while we preached the gospel of God to you" (1 Thess. 2:9), followed by the astonishing confession in his second letter that he has not even eaten their food without paying for it! "On the contrary," he says, "we worked night and day, laboring and toiling so that we would not be a burden to any of you. We did this, not because we do not have the right to such help, but in order to offer ourselves as a model for you to imitate" (2 Thess. 3:7-9).

In these letters, Paul did not identify the nature of his work, but when he arrived in Corinth he met Aquila and Priscilla, a Jewish couple recently expelled from Rome. As Luke tells the story, "because he was a tentmaker as they were, [Paul] stayed and worked with them" (Acts 18:3). The nature of this work was no doubt that of sewing goat hair into tents for sale in the local bazaars, a trade that Paul had probably learned growing up in Tarsus. Writing to the Corinthians a couple of years later, Paul reminds the believers, "We work hard with our own hands" (1 Cor. 4:12), and then in his second letter to the same church he says, "I have labored and toiled and have often gone without sleep" (2 Cor. 11:27). Finally, when saying goodbye to the elders of Ephesus in Miletus Paul reminded them, "You yourselves know that these hands of mine have supplied my own needs and the needs of my companions. In everything I did, I showed you that by this kind of hard work we must help the weak, remembering the words the Lord Jesus himself said: 'It is more blessed to give than to receive'" (Acts 20:34-35).

In these passages we see Paul giving several reasons for his tent-making policy: not to be a burden, to be an example or model of industry and meaningful work, to be able to contribute to others rather than to take from others, and to help the weak. Paul knew very well that he and every Christian worker had the right to be supported financially, yet he refused to take advantage of this right for a very important reason: instead of using this right, he says, "we put up with anything rather than hinder the gospel of Christ" (1 Cor. 9:12). And a few sentences later on in the same passage, he asks, "What then is my reward?" Echoing 2 Thessalonians 3:9, he answers, "Just this: that in preaching the gospel I may offer it free of charge, and so not make full use of my rights as a preacher of the gospel" (1 Cor. 9:18). In other words, all the way through his concern is for the gospel and the integrity of his witness. Although it is true that Paul did receive financial support from Philippi while ministering in Corinth (cf. Phil. 4:15; 2 Cor. 11:9), he never received help from the people he was actually serving at the time. This gave him freedom in speaking, not needing to please the ears of his hearers. Paul wanted no commercialism to enter his relationship with the churches he founded and nurtured (cf. 2 Cor. 12:14).

As for Priscilla and Aquila, they were already full-time tentmakers when Paul met them in Corinth. Very quickly, it appears, they became close friends, so much so that when Paul left Corinth to return to Jerusalem, they accompanied him across the Aegean Sea to Ephesus and stayed there when Paul continued his journey eastward (Acts 18:18-19). While resident in Ephesus, the couple played a critical role in explaining "the way of God more adequately" to the itinerant evangelist Apollos (Acts 18:24-26). When Paul returned to Ephesus on his third missionary journey they continued by his side, even to the point of risking their lives for him in some threatening situation (Rom. 16:4). Later still we find Paul greeting them in Rome as leaders of a house church (Rom. 16:5). Little wonder that Paul included this professional couple — a couple in which Priscilla seems to have taken the leading role in spiritual instruction — among his special circles of "coworkers" (Rom. 16:3).

The Rationale for Tent-making Work

Given the fact that the Greek world viewed manual work as a curse and fit only for slaves, how was it that Paul, Aquila, and Priscilla seem to have adopted a radically different attitude? This can only be explained by their Jewish background, since the Jews saw work as holy and God-like. After all, according to Jewish tradition, God makes things like an artisan. God categorizes and names things as a scientist; carefully plans one process after another; examines the outcome of working, offering quality control; clearly defines each component's function as an engineer; defines humankind's role and provides resources as a good manager; and takes pleasure in work. As a result, the rabbis all had a trade that they pursued alongside the study and teaching of Torah. A father who fails to teach his son a trade, they said, is teaching him to be a thief. Therefore, as R. F. Hock notes in his extensive study of Paul as a tentmaker, Paul's tent-making work was not merely a way of "putting bread (or rice) on the table" so he could do the really important work of preaching. Tent-making was part and parcel of his apostleship — a fully integrated statement of what the gospel of the kingdom of God is about: the transformation of all of life.[2]

As we have seen, there were powerful reasons for Paul and his friends Aquila and Priscilla to engage in this kind of manual work in the first century. But there are good reasons for the model to be reinvented today when church ministry and mission work have become almost totally professionalized.

Consider this example: Virginia is the CEO of a huge micro-development organization in the Philippines. She manages over five thousand employees who serve over a million of the poor, those living on less than one U.S. dollar a day. But she is also an elder of an independent Baptist church, a small church without a lot of rich people to pay the bills. In her engagement with the church she was able to persuade the congregation that "the pastor should work." Even though the church was poor, it could nonetheless fully support their pastor with a living; initially, therefore, Virginia's suggestion met a lot of resistance for reasons that are understandable. Deep within the psyche of religious people is the feeling that men and women of God must not soil their hands and hearts with dirty work in the world, that they are "separated for the Word of God and prayer," that they are a special breed of Christian with a unique, secret call that sets them apart from the

2. R. F. Hock, *The Social Context of Paul's Ministry: Tentmaking and Apostleship* (Philadelphia: Fortress Press, 1980), p. 166.

rest of the people who have not had, or so it is thought, a "special" call. But after this Philippine church endorsed the pastor to work in a microfinance institution, she could say, "I thank God because our pastor sees the real world, enjoying his work and mentoring three hundred poor women entrepreneurs." It is not a new idea.

On the contrary, deep within the biblical tradition there is a strong endorsement of the holiness of work. George Eliot's first novel, *Adam Bede,* set in early nineteenth-century England, presents the carpenter Adam Bede reflecting on how the worker is as near to God as the preacher.

> But t' hear some o' them preachers you'd think as a man must be doing nothing all 's life but shutting 's eyes and looking what's a-going on inside him. I know a man must have the love o' God in his soul, and the Bible's God's word. But what does the Bible say? Why, it says as God put his sperrit [Spirit] into the workman as built the tabernacle, to make him do all the carved work and things as wanted a nice hand. And this is my way o' looking at it: there's the sperrit o' God in all things and all times — weekday as well as Sunday — and i' the great works and inventions, and i' the figuring and the mechanics. And God helps us with our head-pieces and our hands as well as with our souls; and if a man does bits o' jobs out o' working hours — builds a oven for 's wife to save her from going to the bakehouse, or scrats at his bit o' garden and makes two potatoes grow istead o' one, he's doing more good, and he's just as near to God, as if he was running after some preacher and a-praying and a-groaning.[3]

Perhaps this is the reason why, in George MacDonald's novel *The Curate's Awakening,* Mr. Polworth makes this fascinating proposal:

> The great evil in the church has always been the presence in it of persons unsuited for the work required of them there. One

---

3. George Eliot, *Adam Bede* (Ware, U.K.: Wordsworth Editions Ltd., 1997), p. 5.

very simple sifting rule would be, that no one should be admitted to the clergy who had not first proved himself capable of making a better living in some other calling. . . . I would have no one ordained till after forty, by which time he would know whether he had any real call or only a temptation to the church from the hope of an easy living.[4]

But when all is said and done, tent-making is not easy work. Not every form of work is suitable for people who also have a major involvement in church-related ministry or mission work, although I know of a practicing lawyer who serves as the senior pastor of a mid-sized church. Personally, for seven years I combined carpentry and church-planting. I understand what it is like to have, as it seems, three full-time jobs — church, family, and work. Balancing work, ministry, and family is a constant juggling act. While tentmakers may regard their work and ministry as nicely integrated, the people they serve may have the old mentality of the superiority of ministry. Indeed, the tentmaker may struggle with this herself. But there are some advantages. Few tentmakers ever burn out, perhaps because the rhythm of constantly moving between work and ministry is itself life-giving. Someday, in the new heaven and new earth, we may have the opportunity to interview tentmakers, because just as in the first three centuries of church history, in some places in the world today most pastors are tentmakers.[5]

For Discussion and Reflection

If you know of any tentmakers, interview two of them to discover what pressures they face, with what attitude and meaning they ap-

---

4. George MacDonald, *The Curate's Awakening* (Minneapolis: Bethany House Publishers, 1985), pp. 189-90. Permission granted for the quotation.

5. See R. Paul Stevens, "Tentmaking," in Robert Banks and R. Paul Stevens, eds., *The Complete Book of Everyday Christianity* (Downers Grove, Ill.: InterVarsity Press, 1997), pp. 1028-34.

proach their daily work, and whether their daily work contributes to or detracts from their ministry in the church or mission field. Note: Many people may be surprised to discover that they are "tentmakers" since up till now the term has been associated almost exclusively with overseas missionaries in restricted access countries.

The Puritan William Perkins once said that every person needs two strings to his or her bow, referring to the need of a back-up, replacement string in a set of bow-and-arrows. In what way would having a second capacity for daily work be a sign of lacking faith, and in what way could it be an expression of genuine faith? Is it practical in today's world? If not, why?

19

Lasting Work — Paul

Are we creating and cultivating things that have a chance of furnishing the New Jerusalem?

Ben Witherington III

The old saying runs deep in our veins: "Only one life, 'twill soon be past; only what's done for Christ will last." The saying contains a deep truth that we will explore in this chapter, but it also raises the fundamental question, What kind of work done for Christ is it that will last? The popularly understood answer to that question is that only overtly Christian work, such as evangelism or Bible teaching will last. But can that be true? What about other kinds of work? Will they not last at all? Moreover, it is not just Christians who ask whether our life's work has enduring value.

While some people believe we are heading into a new world order and paradise on earth, most people nurse a deep foreboding about the future or refuse to think about it more than they must. Years ago Lesslie Newbigin made the point that much of humankind is "without conviction about any worthwhile end to which

---

Portions of this chapter were published in R. Paul Stevens, *Seven Days of Faith: Every Day Alive with God* (Colorado Springs: Navpress, 2001), pp. 43-51.

the travail of history might lead."[1] The seeming aimlessness of history erodes the nerve of modern people, even of some Christians who should have more reason to embrace the future than anyone. Whether such world-weariness and future fright comes from the terrifying prospect of ecological doomsday, or, as in the case of some Christians who, like the Thessalonians, refused to work in the conviction of Jesus' imminent return, the result for many Christians is the same: all work in this world, except so-called ministry, is not deemed very significant or enduring.

What then is enduring work, work that will last?

Biblical Reflections on Work that Lasts

First, the coming of God in Jesus, his resurrection from the dead, and the gift of God's Spirit on the Day of Pentecost — these are not only the guarantee of the meaningfulness of matter and work, but they are also proof-positive of a glorious future for creation and God's people. The Word became flesh. This means that dualism, the prioritizing of spirit as "good" and matter as "evil," is dead wrong. Christ's first coming in the flesh demonstrates that our future is material as well as spiritual and points to what final redemption will look like. Similarly, his resurrection from the dead guarantees that we will survive in a greatly improved form. The most remarkable aspect of Jesus' resurrected body was his scars — scars that, though now transfigured along with the rest of his physical body into something truly beautiful, nonetheless bore historical continuity with his life in the flesh and the body that ascended to heaven. What a powerful, evocative biblical symbol of the way this life is connected to the next life! Finally, the pouring out of the Spirit was not just empowerment for living and working fruitfully in the here-and-now, but in fact it signaled the irruption of the age to come, the in-breaking of the future into the present. The Spirit's activity, therefore, can be seen in the human,

---

1. Lesslie Newbigin, *Honest Religion for Secular Man* (Philadelphia: Westminster Press, 1966), p. 46.

tangible, material sphere as much as in the spiritual. Speaking to this, John Haughey says, "The future reign is already here but it is here in the way yeast is, hidden in the massive lump of the world. What are we to do? We are to knead eternity into the world until it becomes inextricable from it and both share the same destiny."[2] In light of all this, the most important century for governing our life and priorities is not the first but the last.

Second, the New Testament view of the future of planet earth is not annihilation through nuclear or environmental holocaust, but total renewal. The passage in 2 Peter 3:10 about the heavens disappearing in a roar and the elements being destroyed by fire is often taken to mean that the earth will be annihilated. But this is actually a metaphor of mineral ore being put in a hot cauldron and having the dross burned out (cf. 3:12). Moreover, the text is immediately followed by the statement that we wait for a new heaven and a new earth (3:13). If everything is going up in smoke then it doesn't matter what we do with planet earth; but if God's intention is that the earth be redeemed, along with people, it matters very much what we do with this planet. Putting it differently, if it is true, as the poet Elizabeth Browning suggests, that earth is crammed with heaven (that is, that the realm of God infiltrates our daily life and work now), then is also true that heaven is crammed with earth (we make our marks on heaven and are investing in heaven right now). In his letter to the Romans Paul says that the earth groans now waiting for its full redemption (Rom. 8:22). Yves Congar, one of the theological architects of Vatican II, said, "Ontologically, this is the world that, transformed and renewed, will pass into the kingdom; so . . . the dualist position is wrong; final salvation will be achieved by a wonderful refloating of our earthly vessel rather than the transfer of the survivors to another ship wholly built by God."[3]

Third, the issue of work that lasts is addressed head-on in

---

2. John Haughey, *Converting Nine to Five: A Spirituality of Daily Work* (New York: Crossroad, 1989), p. 104.

3. Yves Congar, *Lay People in the Church: A Study for a Theology of the Laity,* trans. D. Attwater (Westminster, Md.: Newman Press, 1957), p. 92.

three important passages in Paul's first letter to the Corinthians. In the first of these passages, 1 Corinthians 3:12-15, Paul writes, "If anyone builds on this foundation [Christ] . . . their work will be shown for what it is, because the Day will bring it to light. It will be revealed with fire, and the fire will test the quality of each person's work. If what has been built survives, the builder will receive a reward. If it is burned up, the builder will suffer loss but yet will be saved — even though only as one escaping through the flames." Here the apostle makes the sobering point that although some of our work will "pass the durability test," there will be those whose work will not pass the test, though they themselves will be saved, even if only "as [those] escaping through flames."

In the next passage, 1 Corinthians 13:13, Paul writes the famous words, "And now these three remain: faith, hope, and love" — the same triad of marketplace virtues already seen in 1 Thessalonians 1:3. Commenting on this passage in 1 Corinthians, Catholic scholar John Haughey says: "It seems that it is not acts of faith, hope, and love in themselves that last, but rather works done in faith, hope, and love: it is not the pure intention alone, nor is it faith, hope, and love residing unexercised as three infused theological virtues in a person that last. What lasts is the action taken on these virtues, the praxis that flows from the intention, the works the virtues shape. These last!"[4]

Then, in 1 Corinthians 15:58, at the end of his exposition of the practical implications of Jesus' resurrection and our future resurrection, Paul exhorts the Corinthians, "Always give yourselves fully to the work of the Lord, because you know that your labor in the Lord is not in vain." Admittedly, Paul's reference in this passage to "the work of the Lord" pointed to the various ministries engaged in by the Corinthian believers. But even these included such mundane things as "helping" and "administrating." In a wider application of the chapter, Paul is assuring his friends that what makes all their labor — whether homemaking or bridge-building — worthwhile and enduring is the fact that it is done "in the Lord." Speaking to this hopeful text in 1 Corinthians

4. Haughey, *Converting Nine to Five*, p. 106.

15:58 — that our labor in the Lord is not in vain — Alan Richardson comments:

> It is not the secular value or the lasting achievement of our working lives upon earth which gives to our work its Christian significance; it is the final, eschatological reference within it to the heavenly goal that invests it with ultimate worth and meaning. This world will perish, yet nevertheless our labour is not in the last resort futile. . . . It is in the resurrection of Christ that we find the final vindication of all the work that we do in this life, our assurance that our toil and struggle and sufferings possess abiding worth: the short "six days" of our working life on earth will be crowned with that heavenly rest wherein we will survey our work and see that it is good.[5]

Making Our Mark on Heaven

Clearly, through our daily work we leave our mark on the cosmos and our environment, on government, culture, neighborhoods, families, and even on the principalities and powers. The Bible hints that in some way beyond our imagination our marks are permanent. The theological truth that undergirds this fascinating and challenging line of exploration is the statement that Christ is the firstborn of all creation (Col. 1:15) and firstborn from the grave (1:18). If Christ is truly the firstborn of all creation and the firstborn from the grave, then all work has eternal consequences, whether homemaking or being a stockbroker. This brings new meaning to those whose toil is located in so-called secular work — in the arts, education, business, politics, the environment, and the home. Not only are ordinary Christians priests of creation past and present; they, along with missionaries, pastors, and Christian educators, are shaping the future of creation in some significant way. This means that we are invited in Christ to leave

---

5. Alan Richardson, *The Biblical Doctrine of Work* (London: SCM Press, 1954), pp. 55-56.

beautiful marks on creation, on the environment, family, city, workplace, and nation.

Unfortunately, humans have also left negative marks on nature and culture — marks that may not be erased by the final conflict and the final consummation of the travail of history at the second coming of Jesus. But even when we cannot totally undo the violence we have committed against the cosmos, we have faith that in Jesus and by God's grace the environmental, social, cultural, and political scars we have left through our work may yet be transfigured in some substantial way. In the same way, the resurrected body of Jesus had scars, but after the resurrection they were not simply the marks of sin but were transfigured into a means of grace and forgiveness to the disciples. "Put your finger here," Jesus said to Thomas, "Stop doubting and believe" (John 20:27).

In a profound passage, Lesslie Newbigin brings this meditation on "Lasting Work" to a resounding close by showing that there is hope of redemption not only for our souls but also for our work:

> We commit ourselves without reserve to all the secular work our shared humanity requires of us, knowing that nothing we do in itself is good enough to form part of that city's building, knowing that everything — from our most secret prayers to our most public acts — is part of that sin-stained human nature that must go down into the valley of death and judgment, and yet knowing that as we offer it up to the Father in the name of Jesus and in the power of the Spirit, it is safe with him and — purged in fire — it will find its place in the holy city at the end.[6]

Thus, it remains profoundly true: "Only one life, 'twill soon be past; only what's done for Christ will last."

---

6. Lesslie Newbigin, *Foolishness to the Greeks: The Gospel and Western Culture* (Grand Rapids: Eerdmans, 1986), p. 136.

For Discussion and Reflection

The exact way that the New Jerusalem will be furnished by our labors in this life is clearly something beyond what we can imagine. What, however, is the value of imagining in faith what aspect of our work will last?

What "marks" do you wish to make on the new heaven and new earth, to outlast even this life and this world?

20

Heavenly Work — John

But there is labouring even in Paradise that came and is to come.

C. S. Lewis

For children, work and play are one. It is only through the process of growing up that work and play become separated, usually with work taking over almost everything else, even Sabbath. Richard Bolles argues that we live wrongly in three life boxes: the first period — all study; the second — all work; and the third — an orgy of leisure in retirement. What we need, he argues, is a lifelong mix of all three. It is rare to achieve that in this life. But the vision we have of the new heaven and new earth given to us by John the apostle, a prisoner for the Lord on the island of Patmos, is just that: a constant regimen of learning and playful work.[1] The Christian hope for the future is not to be a disembodied soul floating in the ether of heaven. Much more than "saved souls," we will be fully resurrected bodies in a new heaven and new earth, a totally transfigured creation.

1. For an imaginative account of John's life and work see "The Heavenly-Minded Prisoner," in R. Paul Stevens and Alvin Ung, *Taking Your Soul to Work: Overcoming the Nine Deadly Sins of the Workplace* (Grand Rapids: Eerdmans, 2010), pp. 166-68.

In the previous chapter on "Lasting Work" we looked at the question of whether some of our work will last and contribute to the new heaven and new earth. For instance, we could ask whether a software program full of bugs (an obvious one comes to mind!) will survive the final fire or whether it will be purged of all its flaws and find its place in the happy computer carrels lined along the golden streets. We do not know. But we do know that even if some flawed work might survive in the new heaven and new earth (because the future is not the total annihilation of this present creation and our work within it), there will certainly be no curse there, for everything will be transformed by God. Popular belief claims that this whole world is going up in smoke while the saints have been evacuated from it to enjoy a spiritual future in a brand new creation wholly made by God. But why would God destroy what God has lovingly made? In contrast with this pessimistic view of work and creation, the Christian view of the future is that God refloats this earthly vessel wholly renewed rather than transferring the survivors and their work to another lifeboat.

Will We Work in Heaven?

In this chapter on John's vision of the new heaven and the new earth we will look at another urgent question, namely whether we ourselves will work in the new heaven and the new earth. Several considerations suggest a positive answer to this question.

First, there are strong theological reasons for believing that both God and we will be working in the new heaven and new earth. God has certainly not stopped working, nor is God about to stop. Would the Sovereign One stop being God just because the human story on earth has been completed? How could God do that? On the contrary, we expect the Creator to be as creative as when God started to make this universe. This means that God will still be active in sustaining and embellishing the new heaven and new earth. All this has implications for us as well. It is often thought that in this life we human beings worship and evangelize but that in heaven we will just be endlessly worshiping God, singing the same songs over and over. Instead, there are strong reasons for believing that we will not only worship in heaven but also work. It all has to do with the nature of God and the nature of human beings created in the image of God. As God works, so do we; as God loves, so do we; as God sends, so do we. As God is always going outside of God's self, loving, evangelizing, and working, so we can expect the same to be true for us. We must remember that work was given before sin and therefore before the need for redemption. In the new heaven and new earth, will we stop exercising dominion? Stop caring for creation? Stop serving our neighbor? That would mean we would stop being human! Rather, in that new order of things we can expect people to be *more* human rather than less. In light of all these considerations, work must be part of our consummated humanity in the life to come.

Second, God's word gives us textual reasons for believing that we will work in the life to come. Revelation says that "the kings of the earth will bring their splendor into [the holy city]" and that the "glory and honor of the nations will be brought into it" (Rev. 21:24, 26). What can these "glories" be? Probably the best of culture, crafts, commerce, communication, art, music, and technology. The language is similar to the vision of Isaiah, who saw "the wealth on the seas" and "the riches of the nations" being brought to the restored Zion, including herds of camels bearing gold and incense (Isa. 60:5-6). The National Museum in Taipei, Taiwan, houses most of the treasures of six thousand years of Chinese artisanship. It is easy to imagine that incredible jade bowls, ceramics, and enameled vessels of the type found in that place will also be in the New Jerusalem, even with their exquisite calligraphy. N. T. Wright wonders what musical instruments we will have to play in God's new world, but he is sure that Bach's music will be there![2] Perhaps even automobiles, cell phones, canoes, designer clothing, handmade quilts, welded picnic tables, gourmet meals, skyscrapers and tents, farms and factories will also be there. And as for governance in the new society, Jesus promised the disciples

2. N. T. Wright, *Surprised by Hope: Rethinking Heaven, the Resurrection, and the Mission of the Church* (New York: HarperOne, 2008), p. 209.

that they would rule with him (Matt. 19:28). In Genesis human beings were made to rule; in Revelation they rule again (Rev. 1:6; 2:26). No wonder, then, that John could say that the deeds of Christians "will follow them" (14:13), not only in the sense that they themselves survive but perhaps even in the sense of continuing to engage in their work.

Third, work in the new heaven and new earth will be all that good work was intended to be. Perhaps what we will be doing is what we have done in this life but without the sweat and frustration experienced here. Perhaps we will do what we have always wanted to do but couldn't, either through lack of time or opportunity. Since there will be no curse on work, the workplace, or the worker, labor will be personally and completely satisfying, far more than was obtainable in this life. Frustrated artists will have full scope for their talents. Town planners will have ample scope for design and implementation. Perhaps there will even be marketing in heaven, since human beings in their uniqueness will produce all kinds of products and services. In George MacDonald's book *The Curate's Awakening,* Polworth shares a vision he has had of doing business in heaven. People are going to stores to get what they need. The loveliest silks and woolens are in one shop. Both customers and shop-keepers are respectful of each other. Yet amazingly, no money is passing hands. Each person gives what he or she has and each person gets what he or she needs, no more and no less. Such is the nature of marketing without the need for profit![3] Moreover, this kingdom work will be culturally diverse with people gathered from every nation, tribe, and language (Rev. 7:9). The Chinese, aboriginals, Germans, English, Latin Americans, and Africans will all bring their unique perspectives on work. In this way, true globalization will finally be achieved with a profound sense of interdependence and a rich engagement in cultural diversity.

Here play and work will be reunited again, as it was with us in childhood. Thankfully, even work and worship will once more be

---

3. George MacDonald, *The Curate's Awakening* (Minneapolis: Bethany House Publishers, 1985), pp. 144-45.

completely one. John's poetic and visionary message has drawn back the veil so we can see things in the Spirit, the way reality is and what it will be like, including our work. Revelation touches us at the point of our despair, our world-weariness, our future shock, our fear of persecution, our collaboration with a sick (even if sometimes friendly) society. Because of this it may well be, as the classic commentator G. B. Caird suggested, that Revelation is the most relevant book of the Bible for this moment in history.[4]

In *Gilead,* a novel by Marilynne Robinson, a father with a terminal illness writes a long letter to his little son, now too young to read his thoughts. With penetrating insight he shares his conviction about the eternal state:

> I can't believe that, when we have all been changed and put on incorruptibility, we will forget our fantastic condition of mortality and impermanence. . . . In eternity this world will be Troy, I believe, and all that has passed here will be the epic of the universe, the ballad they sing in the streets. Because I don't imagine any reality putting this one in the shade entirely, and I think piety forbids me to try.[5]

The future is more than paradise restored. It is creation transfigured — including that of our work.

For Discussion and Reflection

How can you now answer the question, "Why work?"

Reflect on your own answer to the village watchman's question in the following story.

While walking in a neighboring village late one night, a Hassidic rebbe met a man who was also walking alone. For a while, the two walked in silence. Finally, the rebbe turned to the

---

4. G. B. Caird. *The Revelation of St. John the Divine* (New York: Harper & Row, 1966), p. 13.

5. Marilynne Robinson, *Gilead* (New York: Picador, 2004), p. 57.

man and asked, "So, who do you work for?" "I work for the village," the man answered. "I'm the night watchman." They walked in silence again. Finally, the night watchman asked the rebbe, "And who do you work for?" The rebbe answered, "I'm not always sure. But this I will tell you. Name your present salary and I will double it. All you have to do is walk with me and ask me, from time to time, 'Who do you work for?'"[6]

---

6. Jeffrey Salkin, *Being God's Partner: How to Find the Hidden Link between Spirituality and Your Work* (Woodstock, Vt.: Jewish Lights Publishing, 1994), p. 29.

The New Testament: A Brief Summary

The New Testament assumes the high view of the dignity and purpose of human labor in the Old Testament. Unlike those in the Greek world who regarded work as a curse, Christians were inspired to see work in several specific ways:

First, work is good. In some religious systems holy people do not work. But God came in Jesus as a worker and so honored human labor. Followers of Jesus were persuaded by Jesus and the apostles to undertake productive labor to provide for their own needs, to serve others, and to witness to the surrounding culture by their work ethic.

Second, Jesus personally incarnated the realm of God and demonstrated that the coming of that realm was not merely the development of a spiritual state of being but the dynamic rule of God in all of life and all of creation. The coming of God's realm is partly accomplished through good human work. Such labor brings well-being to people, invites relationship with our Creator, creates new wealth, and resists powers that frustrate and distort God's life-giving rule on earth. So work for God's realm means the end of dualism, namely that certain kinds of work are holy and spiritual (such as the work of pastors and missionaries) and other kinds of labor are secular.

Third, the story of Mary and Martha demonstrates that work should be contemplative. Our daily labor must not become an alternative to attending to the presence of God. Indeed our work can become an opportunity to meditate, to pray, to grow spiritually, to serve others, and to love God.

Fourth, because of the resurrection of Christ and the descent of the Spirit, our work "in the Lord" is not in vain. Our future is not to be disembodied souls but resurrected persons. Some of our work undertaken with faith, hope, and love will last and even outlast this world, contributing in some way to the new heaven and new earth.

Fifth, in Genesis human beings were commissioned to rule over everything; in the last book of the Bible men and women in Christ are made a "kingdom and priests" undertaking the stewardship and the development of creation and human communities in an environment free of sin and the curse. This biblical vision of the past, present, and future of work inspires us to do our work well and to work for the Sovereign who is the ultimate recipient of our labor.

Epilogue: How Then Shall We Work?

I am writing this in my seventy-third year of life. As I reflect on my life journey I see that most of my work was good: building a lathe, developing black and white photographs in the dark room, along with designing and building a photographic enlarger using my old bellows camera, building a speed boat, and designing and constructing a cabinet for our sound system. Then there was all that work as a student at school and university, work for which there was no financial remuneration. Just the reverse. Some of that school work, I fear, was done for the wrong motive, to gain approval, and I now wonder if anything of it will endure. More recently I have done some work at home — maintenance (not a lot, my wife is quick to add) and chores like washing up after the meals. I have been a pastor, a carpenter, a student counselor, a bookkeeper, a professor, an academic dean, and now a refusing-to-be-retired self-employed consultant. Meanwhile, through the years I have been a son, husband, father, and grandfather. There was some play in these roles but certainly a lot of work as well. Was all of this good work? Was it good work even when I deeply wounded a colleague and ruptured a relationship with someone with whom I was building a new community? And this book! Will it last? I trust it is good work and edifying to those who read it. But what if it misleads or contains errors?

At various periods of its history, starting in about the third century, the church has had lists of prohibited occupations. In

Robert Grant's research the list includes rich persons who shut people up in prisons or oppress the poor; painters of pictures, especially makers of idols; workers in silver and bronze who are thieves; dishonest tax collectors; those who alter weights and measures; innkeepers who mix water with their wine; soldiers who act lawlessly; charioteers and gladiators, prostitutes and pimps, astrologists and magicians. From this list it appears that some of the occupations are not prohibited in themselves but only if they are practiced immorally.[1] All this raises important questions: can "good" work be done badly and can not-so-good work be done with good motives and for the benefit of others? It also raises the question of how one performs good work in an unjust system.

Jesus' way of dealing with unjust systems can teach us many things. Certainly there was corruption and an unjust tax system in first-century Palestine. In this situation Jesus modeled shrewdness and applied different solutions in different contexts. For instance, he removed Matthew the tax collector from the system but encouraged another tax collector, Zacchaeus, to stay in the system while not forgetting to practice justice and to repay with interest those whom he had defrauded. On another occasion Jesus himself paid taxes to Caesar while insisting that we should render to Caesar what belongs to Caesar and to God what belongs to God. We see, therefore, that withdrawal, transformation, and discerning participation are all viable options for our dealings with a fallen system. How to decide what to do in any given circumstance requires shrewdness, sometimes called "wisdom" in the Bible. Shrewdness means seizing an opportunity to advance the rule of God in whatever way we can in our given circumstances — that is, doing the best we can in an imperfect situation.

In answer to the question how we are to work in the real world — in Cain's world, in the city that he built — we can also be helped by reflecting on things previously emphasized in this study.

First, we work in faith — that is, in fellowship with God, like

---

1. Robert M. Grant, "Work and Occupations," in *Early Christianity and Society* (New York: Harper & Row Publishers, 1977), pp. 85-87.

Abel and many of the leading figures whose work-lives we have examined. We work for God. We work knowing that far from being a hindrance to spiritual growth, work provides a context for soul growth.

Second, we work in love, fellowship, and interdependence with coworkers, building community in every way we can. Our work is a practical way of loving our neighbors, near and far, as well as providing for our family and loved ones close to home.

Third, we work in hope, engaging the powers that frustrate God's life-giving realm on earth, and being persuaded that some of our work will last and contribute to the new heaven and new earth. Reinhold Niebuhr summarizes all of this in a thoughtful — and for us, closing — reflection:

> Nothing that is worth doing can be achieved in our lifetime; therefore we must be saved by hope. Nothing which is true and beautiful or good makes complete sense in any immediate context of history; therefore we must be saved by faith. Nothing we do, however virtuous, can be accomplished alone; therefore we are saved by love. No virtuous act is quite as virtuous from the standpoint of our friend or foe as it is from our standpoint. Therefore we must be saved by the final form of love which is forgiveness.[2]

---

2. Quoted in Os Guiness, *The Call: Finding and Fulfilling the Central Purpose of Your Life* (Nashville: Word Publishing, 1998), p. 243.

Selected Bibliography: Theology of Work

Bakke, Dennis W. *Joy at Work: A Revolutionary Approach to Fun on the Job.* Seattle: PVG, 2005.

Bakke, Ray, Lowell Bakke, and William Hendricks. *Joy at Work Bible Study Companion.* Seattle: PVG, 2005.

Banks, Robert. *God the Worker: Journeys into the Mind, Heart, and Imagination of God.* Valley Forge, Pa.: Judson Press, 1994.

Banks, Robert, and Kimberly Powell, eds. *Faith in Leadership: How Leaders Live Out Their Faith in Their Work and Why It Matters.* San Francisco: Jossey-Bass, 2000.

Beckett, John D. *Loving Monday: Succeeding in Business without Losing Your Soul.* Expanded ed. Downers Grove, Ill.: InterVarsity Press, 2006.

————. *Mastering Monday: A Guide to Integrating Faith and Work.* Downers Grove, Ill.: InterVarsity Press, 2006.

Bernbaum, John A., and Simon Steer. *Why Work? Careers and Employment in Biblical Perspective.* Grand Rapids: Baker Book House, 1986.

Bernstein, Peter L. *Against the Gods: The Remarkable Story of Risk.* New York: John Wiley and Sons, 1996.

Block, Peter. *Stewardship: Choosing Service Over Self-Interest.* San Francisco: Berrett-Koehler, 1993.

Capon, Robert Farrar. *An Offering of Uncles: The Priesthood of Adam and the Shape of the World.* New York: Crossroad, 1982.

Congar, Yves. *Lay People in the Church: A Study for a Theology of the Laity.* Trans. D. Attwater. Westminster Md.: Newman Press, 1957.

Cosden, Darrell. *The Heavenly Good of Earthly Work.* Peabody, Mass.: Hendrickson, 2006.

————. *A Theology of Work: Work and the New Creation.* Carlisle, Cumbria, U.K.: Paternoster Press, 2004.

Costa, John Dalla. *Magnificence at Work: Living Faith in Business.* Ottawa: Saint Paul University — Novalis Press, 2005.

Crawford, Matthew B. *Shop Class as Soul Craft: An Inquiry into the Value of Work.* New York: Penguin Press, 2009.

Crouch, Andrew. *Culture Making: Recovering Our Creative Calling.* Downers Grove, Ill.: InterVarsity Press, 2008.

Curran, Peter. *All the Hours God Sends? Practical and Biblical Help in Meeting the Demands of Work.* Leicester, U.K.: InterVarsity Press, 2000.

de Botton, Alain. *The Pleasures and Sorrows of Work.* New York: Pantheon Books, 2009.

Diehl, William E. *Thank God It's Monday.* Philadelphia: Fortress Press, 1982.

—————. *The Monday Connection: A Spirituality of Competence, Affirmation, and Support in the Workplace.* San Francisco: HarperSanFrancisco, 1991.

Diehl, William E., and Judith Ruhe Diehl. *It Ain't Over Till It's Over.* Minneapolis: Augsburg Books, 2003.

Droel, William L. *Business People: The Spirituality of Work.* Chicago: ACTA Publications, 1990.

Dumbrell, William. "Creation, Covenant, and Work." *Crux* 24, no. 3 (September 1988): 14-24.

Grant, Robert M. "Work and Occupations." In *Early Christianity and Society.* New York: Harper & Row Publishers, 1977.

Graves, Stephen R., and Thomas G. Addington. *The Fourth Frontier: Exploring the New World of Work.* Nashville: Word, 2000.

Green, Thomas H. *Darkness in the Marketplace: The Christian at Prayer in the World.* Notre Dame, Ind.: Ave Maria Press, 1981.

Greene, Mark. *The Great Divide.* London: The London Institute for Contemporary Christianity, 2010.

Greenleaf, Robert K. *Servant Leadership: A Journey into the Nature of Legitimate Power and Greatness.* New York: Paulist Press, 1977.

Griffiths, Brian. *The Creation of Wealth: A Christian's Case for Capitalism.* Downers Grove, Ill.: InterVarsity, 1984.

Guiness, Os. *The Call: Finding and Fulfilling the Central Purpose of Your Life.* Nashville: Word, 1998.

Hammond, Pete, R. Paul Stevens, and Todd Svanoe. *The Marketplace Annotated Bibliography: A Christian Guide to Books on Work, Business, and Vocation.* Downers Grove, Ill.: InterVarsity Press, 2002.

Hardy, Lee. *The Fabric of This World: Inquiries into Calling, Career Choice, and the Design of Human Work.* Grand Rapids: Eerdmans, 1990.

Haughey, John. *Converting Nine to Five: A Spirituality of Daily Work.* New York: Crossroad, 1989.

Heiges, Donald R. *The Christian's Calling.* Philadelphia: United Lutheran Church in America, 1958.

Helgesen, Sally. *The Female Advantage: Women's Ways of Leadership.* New York: Doubleday, 1990.

Higginson, Richard. *Questions of Business Life: Exploring Workplace Issues from a Christian Perspective.* Carlisle, Cumbria, U.K.: Spring Harvest, 2002.

————. *Called to Account: Adding Value in God's World: Integrating Christianity and Business Effectively.* Glasgow: HarperCollins, 1993.

Hock, R. F. *The Social Context of Paul's Ministry: Tentmaking and Apostleship.* Philadelphia: Fortress Press, 1980.

Holland, Joe. *Creative Communion: Toward a Spirituality of Work.* New York: Paulist Press, 1989.

Jensen, David H. *Responsive Labor: A Theology of Work.* Louisville: Westminster John Knox Press, 2006.

Killinger, Barbara. *Workaholics: The Respectable Addicts.* New York: Simon and Schuster, 1991.

Kraemer, Hendrik. *A Theology of the Laity.* Philadelphia: Westminster Press, 1958.

Larive, Armand. *After Sunday: A Theology of Work.* New York: Continuum, 2004.

Marshall, Paul. *A Kind of Life Imposed on Man: Vocation and Social Order from Tyndale to Locke.* Toronto: University of Toronto Press, 1996.

————. *Thine Is the Kingdom.* Grand Rapids: Eerdmans, 1986.

Marshall, Paul, with Lela Gilbert. *Heaven Is Not My Home: Learning to Live in God's Creation.* Nashville: Word, 1998.

Meilaender, Gilbert C., ed. *Working: Its Meaning and Its Limits.* Notre Dame, Ind.: University of Notre Dame Press, 2000.

Miller, David W. *God at Work: The History and Promise of the Faith at Work Movement.* New York: Oxford University Press, 2006.

Minear, Paul. "Work and Vocation in Scripture." In *Work and Vocation,* edited by J. Nelson. New York: Harper, 1954.

Nicholls, Bruce. *Contextualization: A Theology of Gospel and Culture.* Downers Grove, Ill.: InterVarsity Press, 1979.

Norris, Kathleen. *Acedia and Me: A Marriage, Monks, and a Writer's Life* New York: Penguin Books, 2008.

Novak, Michael. *Business as a Calling: Work and the Examined Life.* New York: The Free Press, 1996.

————. *Toward a Theology of the Corporation.* Washington: American Enterprise Institute for Public Policy Research, 1982.

Perkins, William. "A Treatise of the Vocations or Callings of Men." In *The Work of William Perkins,* edited and introduced by Ian Breward. Abingdon, U.K.: Sutton Courtenay Press, 1970.

Preece, Gordon. *Changing Work Values: A Christian Response*. Melbourne: Acorn Press, 1995.

Richardson, Alan. *The Biblical Doctrine of Work*. London: SCM Press, 1954.

Rifkin, Jeremy. *The End of Work: The Decline of the Global Work-Force and the Dawn of the Post-Market Era*. London: Penguin Books, 2000.

Ryken, Leland. *Redeeming the Time: A Christian Approach to Work and Leisure*. Grand Rapids: Baker, 1995.

Salkin, Jeffrey. *Being God's Partner: How to Find the Hidden Link between Spirituality and Your Work*. Woodstock, Vt.: Jewish Lights Publishing, 1994.

Schmemann, Alexander. *For the Life of the World*. Crestwood, N.Y.: St. Vladimir's Seminary Press, 1988.

Schumacher, Christian. *God in Work: Discovering the Divine Pattern for Work in the New Millennium*. Oxford: Lion Publishing House, 1998.

Sherman, Doug, and William Hendricks. *Your Work Matters to God*. Colorado Springs: Navpress, 1987.

Stackhouse, Max L., and Peter Paris, eds. *God and Globalization*. 2 vols. Harrisburg, Pa.: Trinity Press International, 2000-2007.

Stevens, R. Paul. *Doing God's Business: Meaning and Motivation for the Marketplace*. Grand Rapids: Eerdmans, 2006.

———. *Down-to-Earth Spirituality: Encountering God in the Ordinary, Boring Stuff of Life*. Downers Grove, Ill.: InterVarsity Press, 2003.

———. *The Other Six Days: Vocation, Work, and Ministry in Biblical Perspective*. Grand Rapids: Eerdmans, 1999. Published in the U.K. as *The Abolition of the Laity*.

———. "The Spiritual and Religious Sources of Entrepreneurship: From Max Weber to the New Business Spirituality." *Crux* 36, no 2 (June 2000): 22-33. Reprinted in *Stimulus: The New Zealand Journal of Christian Thought and Practice* 9, no. 1 (Feb. 2001): 2-11.

Stevens, R. Paul, and Robert Banks. *Marketplace Ministry Handbook*. Vancouver: Regent College Publishing, 2005.

Stevens, R. Paul, and Alvin Ung. *Taking Your Soul to Work: Overcoming the Nine Deadly Sins of the Workplace*. Grand Rapids: Eerdmans, 2010.

Tabalujian, Benny. *God on Monday: Reflections on Christians @ Work*. Melbourne, Australia: Klesis Institute, 2005.

Terkel, Studs. *Working: People Talk about What They Do All Day and How They Feel about What They Do*. New York: Ballantine Books, 1974.

Theriault, Reg. *How to Tell When You're Tired: A Brief Examination of Work*. New York: W. W. Norton & Co., 1995.

Ting, John. *Living Biblically at Work*. Singapore: Landmark Books, 1995.

Tournier, Paul. *The Gift of Feeling*. Translated by Edwin Hudson. Atlanta: John Knox Press, 1979.

Veith, Gene E. *God at Work: Your Christian Vocation in All of Life*. Wheaton, Ill.: Crossway, 2002.

Volf, Miroslav. *Work in the Spirit: Toward a Theology of Work*. New York: Oxford University Press, 1991.

————. "Human Work, Divine Spirit, and the New Creation: Toward a Pneumatological Understanding of Work." *Pneuma: The Journal of the Society for Pentecostal Studies* (Fall 1987): 173-93.

Witherington, Ben III. *Work: A Kingdom Perspective on Labor*. Grand Rapids: Eerdmans, 2011.

Wyszynski, Stefan Cardinal. *All You Who Labor: Work and the Sanctification of Daily Life*. Manchester, N.H.: Sophia Institute Press, 1995.

Young, Michael, and Tom Schuller. *Life after Work: The Arrival of the Ageless Society*. London: HarperCollins, 1991.